The Divine Power of

Edited by: Penny Thres

https://www.facebook.com/cornerhousewords

Cover Image & Photography: Natasha Holland, Natasha Holland Photography

https://natashahollandphotography.zenfolio.com/

Creative Coordinator: Leanne MacDonald, Leanne MacDonald Well-Being

https://www.leannemacdonaldwellbeing.com/

Copyright The Inner Feminine Collective 2020

Welcome to the Inner Feminine Collective.

Celebrating powerful women fearlessly stepping into their true purpose and calling.

Thank you, Universe, for guiding your beautiful soul this book.

We are a collective of powerful women whose mission is to co create with the Universe, embodying our unique feminine energy and stepping into our true propose.

It is our mission and souls calling to help, inspire, empower women, just like you, to accept your true calling and true purpose.

Leanne & Natasha xx
Co – Founders, The Inner Feminine Collective

Photo Credit Natasha Holland Photography

Our stories -

Chapter 1   *Life* – **Penny Thresher**

Chapter 2   *Courageous* – **Cheryl Mercer**

Chapter 3   *Acceptance* – **Natasha Holland**

Chapter 4   *Powerful* – **L N Sheffield**

Chapter 5   *Grateful* – **Helen Bartram**

Chapter 6   *Rejuvenation* – **Hazel Carter**

Chapter 7   *Rebirth* - **Denise W Saunders**

Chapter 8   *Connection* – **Kirsty Pearson**

Chapter 9   *Phoenix* – **Amy Whistance**

Copyright The Inner Feminine Collective 2020

Chapter 10	*Intuition* – Michelle Maslin-Taylor
Chapter 11	*Mother* – Gemma Alexander
Chapter 12	*Wisdom* – Jules Sutton
Chapter 13	*Compassion* – Kim Boyd
Chapter 14	*Rising* – Jayne Holland
Chapter 15	*Resilient* – Claire Zorlutuna
Chapter 16	*Choices* – Lisa Johnson
Chapter 17	*Empowerment* – Kerrie Patterson
Chapter 18	*Discovering* – Wendy Concannon
Chapter 19	*Complete* – Vivienne Edgecombe
Chapter 20	*Strong* – Leanne Taylor
Chapter 21	*More* – Mariella O'Brien
Chapter 22	*Freedom* – Wendi May New
Chapter 23	*Learning* – Sara Calgie
Chapter 24	*Hope* – Simone Lanham
Chapter 25	*Survival* – Susan Smalley
Chapter 26	*Truth* – Leanne MacDonald

Chapter 1 - Penny Thresher

Copyright The Inner Feminine Collective 2020

Life is not measured by the number of breaths you take but by the moments that take your breath away

- Maya Angelou

Sometimes I am in total awe of that woman.

I see her strength, her power, her fortitude. I see her keep going no matter what, with love in her heart and fire in her soul.

And then I see her frailty, her fear, her fatigue. I see her sigh as she feels the weight of the world settling on her shoulders. Feels all the feelings.

I see how she hates her neglected body until she remembers. The pleasure it has received and given. That it gave the gift of life, and that birth left its mark on her to remind her everyday of that miracle. The stretch marks record the growth of new life, and the sagging breasts are testament to feeding that child.

I hear her stories. Her life stories. Not just the ones that really happened, but the untold ones she allows to creep into her consciousness at unguarded moments.

I see her struggle. Fight to do the right thing. To get up stronger every time she is knocked down. To keep going no matter what.

But recently, I have seen her rise. She is taller, stronger, braver. She has found her voice and is using it. She is sharing her dreams, her knowledge, her love. She breathes deeply and feels strongly. Secure in the knowledge that what she has discovered must be shared. That every woman is entitled to feel the magic, let go of what is past and stand in her own space, raise her own voice.

She is standing in her power. At last. And she wants other women to do the same.

She is me, of course.

This book is full of stories from women like me. We are all different, and yet we are all the same. When you read them, you will weep with us, and you will laugh too. You will feel our pain, and revel in our joy. You may reflect on your own stories. Become part of the sisterhood that binds us together and leads to us saying to each other. I know you. I see you. I hear you.

Compared to some, my story is not really one of hardship. Yes, there has been difficulty. But I cannot honestly say that there was trauma. At times I have felt resentful, angry, bitter. But if you take all that away, what remains? Love.

I was born in 1958, in North London. Just 13 years after the end of World War II. Looking at the black and white pictures of my childhood I see a sturdy child with laughter in her eyes, peeking out from under a straight fringe. Sometimes solemn, and other times full of joy. With a dog, a cat, a garden. My dad took many photographs. We lived on the ground floor of a Victorian terrace house.

My earliest memory is of a pretty woman with red hair in a chic bun, and wearing a blue dress bending over me in my cot, smiling, and talking in a soft voice. I can remember music and voices in the background. My parents threw many parties. My mum was so beautiful.

When I was 4 my little sister arrived. There are pictures of her and I together, smiling at Dad through the camera. I look proud and a little protective.

I also remember having the measles later that year. I was very ill. My mum was worried for the baby, but she did not catch it. I remember feeling so ill. Laying on the sofa in a darkened room with bamboo wallpaper and a red rug laid over me.

I remember reading with my dad. He was tall and strong and being with him felt safe.

We moved away from London when I was 6. A year in Essex, then to Hertfordshire where I would remain for the next 51 years.

But my family broke apart when I was 16. At a time when divorce was still something rather shameful. The division caused by that event has left all involved slightly damaged, and some of the rifts caused will never be healed. Looking back, I know that it left me feeling adrift, rootless. Deserted. That feeling led to some bad decisions that led me down some dark paths. No excuses, no blame. It was what it was.

I found it hard to trust. Hard to commit. In my mid-twenties I resigned myself to being alone, to not having the children that I so longed for.

But I did find someone. Fell in love. Married. Had a child. The gift of a daughter. A tiny scrap, born wise and full of joy. She had a dog, cats, a garden.

But when she was 6 my marriage fell apart. Ended by addiction. What was in the bottle was more precious than his wife and child. It ended in violence and debt. But my child had brought me into the light, given me something to fight for. A reason to be brave, to lead by example, to keep going.

There was financial hardship. Choices dictated by the effort of keeping the wolf from the door. Choices that felt more like no choice. Leaving me feeling disempowered and pathetic. But while I was focused on the pain, those choices became part of the fabric of my life, leading me somewhere brighter, more beautiful than I could ever imagine. We began to heal.

I stumbled into the secure arms of a man who took everything that we threw at him, my daughter and I, but stood steadfast, wrapped us up in his love and created solid ground for us to launch from. Together the three of us found laughter and joy. Sharing the ups and downs that are part of the experience of life. Each one teaching us something that we needed to learn.

Nearly 20 years later he is still by my side supporting and encouraging. Believing in me even when I do not. He has been a strong father, a loving husband. My daughter has grown into a beautiful young woman, strong and determined. A healer and a carer. She tilts at windmills, defends the people she loves and cares for. She has no idea just how amazing she is.

On balance, I would say my life has been blessed.

Through all of this I was aware that I was searching for something. At the age of 13 I embarked on a quest to discover something to believe in. I did not know then that it was a quest! But I can see that I was looking for some reason for it all. I studied the bible at school and decided it was an amazing work of fiction. A great novel.

I went on to study other religions in great depth. Envious of people who had faith. A conviction that there was a greater power, some omnipotent presence overseeing our lives. But religion caused so much pain too. Started wars and brought conflict. I could not reconcile that with the faith I was searching for.

When I was small, I remember conversations with ghostly white spectral figures, floating about a foot off the floor, that visited me in my bedroom at night. They were beautiful and although I do not remember the conversations in detail, I do remember a sense of safety and joy in their presence.

As I grew older, I no longer saw them, but I often felt them by my side. At various times in my life I have been able to name them. They have sent messages, provided support when asked. Never intrusive, always waiting for an invitation. They change from time to time, depending on what I need. But someone always shows up.

During the hard times I have often forgotten to call on them. But they have never given up on me. They have always known that the time will come when I will beckon them close.

We relocated to Morecambe in the north west of the UK three years ago. A faded majestic English seaside town which has recently begun to climb out of years of decline. I am in another Victorian terrace house; an end terrace this time. The Corner House welcomed us in and enveloped us in a warm embrace. Providing me with somewhere to grow, to start a new business, to breathe.

It has been an interesting 3 years. A very different life, more peaceful, which was what we longed for. But not without some angst!

It began with the discovery of a spiritual understanding that made sense of everything, that gave me the faith that I had been searching for. The knowledge that I was OK. That the universe had my back. I began a gentle journey of exploration that continues and has brought me great contentment and introduced many wonderful people into my life.

But just over a year ago one of our elderly Labradors passed away. Although all dogs are special, Ben was something more. Such wisdom and grace. I was plunged into a maelstrom of grief which opened a door to so much more. A whole year of reflection and reconciliation.

Something stirred inside of me, something that had been slumbering until I was ready. I recognised that I had been trying to fit in somewhere that I did not belong. I had been ignoring the signs all around me. Events conspired to remove the negative energy from my life, and whilst it brought some pain it also opened the door to so much more.

So here she is. That woman. Still strong but frail. Energised but still sometimes fatigued. Fierce but gentle. Loved and loving. Grateful for everything she has and has had. Determined. Occasionally judgemental but working on it!

Finally embracing her power. In the right place at the right time. Helping other women get their stories out into the world. Watching flowers bloom in the sunshine of self-acceptance. Far from perfect but accepting that even her flaws are beautiful because they are part of her. And she has a beautiful heart, filled with compassion, kindness, and love. Which she sends out into the world wholeheartedly.

Remember my Dad? Well he died several years ago. Sadly, we were estranged when he died, and had been for about 10 years. There was a lot of anger and misunderstanding which we never got the opportunity to put right. It has taken me a long time to set that aside and forgive him and myself for not trying harder. For not realising that love overcomes all obstacles. I miss him, more than I thought I would.

Looking back now, I think that my dad was a bit lost. It was not anyone's fault. Like me he was searching for something but did not know it. I think he was looking in the wrong places. He seemed restless, distracted. In the end he found someone who was strong, almost dictatorial. Someone who recognised that he needed a defined path. I believe that sometimes he missed the freedom of his wandering, and the life he left behind. There was so much pain and sadness centred around his choice. It took me a long time to forgive.

He was a typesetter and worked in the newspaper industry for years before starting his own company called Expert Composition. In those days, before computers, he composed on a Linotype machine. The words were typed in on a keyboard which dropped brass keys down into a holder and then an impression would be made in hot metal. The cast would then be laid out in a wooden holder in "galleys" which would be inked and then impressed onto paper.

I grew up proof reading with him, as well as reading. He inspired in me my love of words. Which led to me reading and writing all my life. Recently I have realised that this is my real passion. Words come easily to me. They roll onto the paper, alive and kicking, demanding to be read.

When I read other people's words, I feel them, I see meaning in them, see the stories behind the words. Words are my thing.

In recent weeks I have, somewhat magically, rediscovered my connection with my dad.

Soon after we moved to Morecambe a medium told me that someone called John was with me. He also mentioned the name Harold. This person wanted to tell me that he was proud of me. That wished he had told me when he could. That he knew that he could have done things better.

My dad's name was John Harold Hills. And I realised that I knew he was with me. I feel his presence over my shoulder when I am writing. He has joined my "team" of advisors, of supporters. If I need him, he is there. I forgave him a while ago, perhaps that is why he felt able to reconnect.

I have begun to trust the magic. The mysterious alchemy of spirit and love that ignites passion and lights the blue touch paper of creativity. Words flow and I see beauty all around me.

I have always felt deeply and passionately about things. My feelings, both good and bad burn hot inside me and explode randomly, sometimes awkwardly, but usually in a glorious burst of spiritual energy that explodes out of me and showers sparks over anyone in my immediate vicinity.

It can be triggered by words, by music, a photograph, a beach, or a sunset. When I am in flow EVERYTHING triggers me. It can be overwhelming, but it is a reminder of the glorious fucking mess that we call life.

So, what do I want to leave you with from my story?

How about 5 things I have learned about life and living?

Forgive

…sincerely, with no expectation of anything in return. Remember everyone is doing the best they can with the tools they have available at the time.

Be kind

…kindness costs nothing and yet is like a rare precious metal, a priceless commodity that accumulates and grows exponentially

Connect

…connection is what binds us together, its incredibly powerful. There is nothing we cannot achieve if we are connected. It is essential for our health and wellbeing. Reach out for it, recognise it when it reaches out for you. Embrace it!

Love

…wholeheartedly and unreservedly. Even when it is not reciprocated. Even when it is thrown back in your face. Love IS the answer!

Live

…Life is not a rehearsal. Don't wait. Grab it by the throat and live it. Make every second count.

Penny Thresher
Corner House Coaching

Chapter 2 - Cheryl Mercer

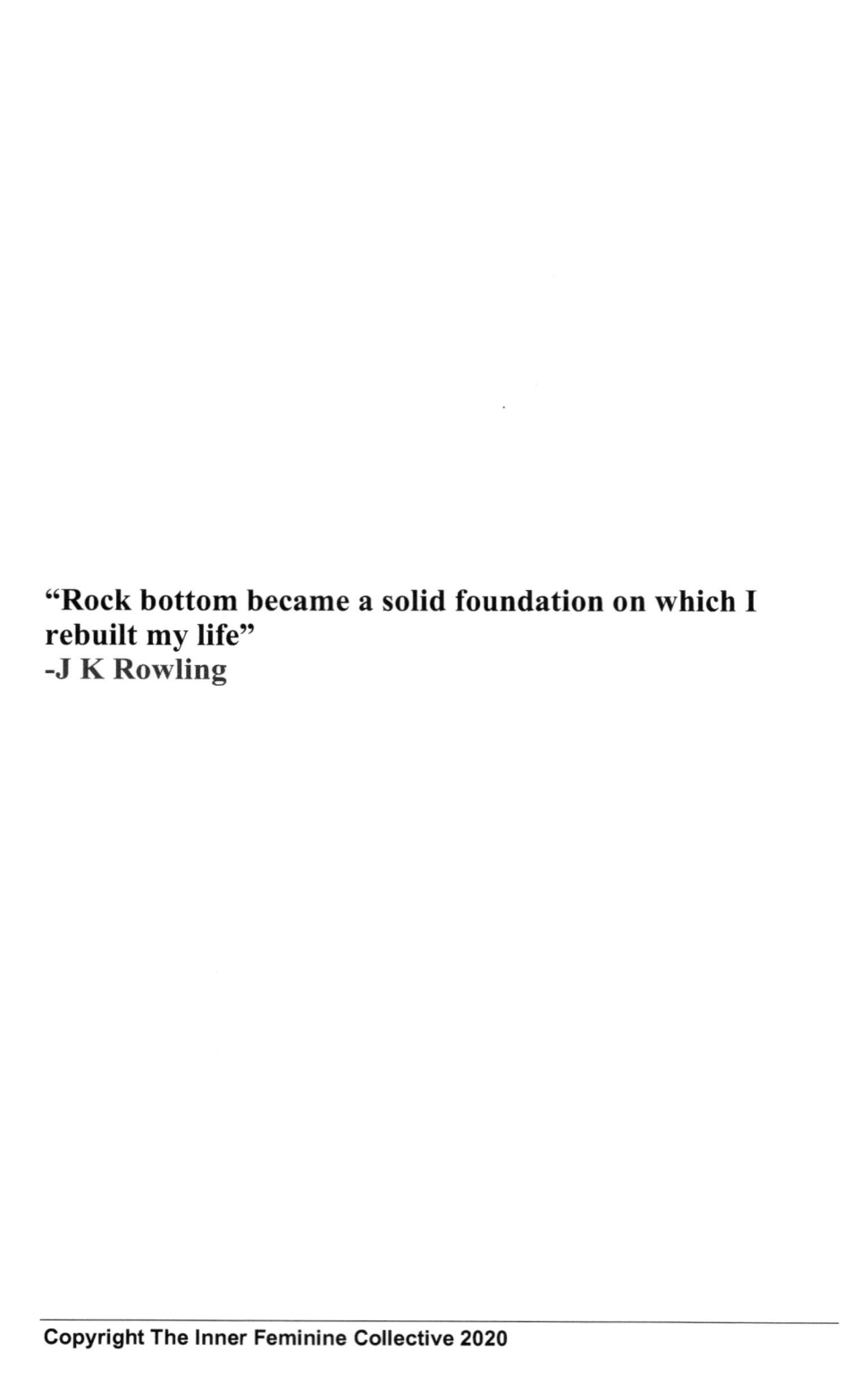

"Rock bottom became a solid foundation on which I rebuilt my life"
-J K Rowling

The Missing Piece

A little about me. I am a thinker, dreamer, soul seeker, resilient, strong warrior, and action taker. But I have not always been this way. I became this woman after hitting the self-destruct button six years ago.

All my life I was told that I was not enough, not worthy. That I would never amount to anything. I was too sensitive, too much. I allowed the critics to win. I hid from life and played small. It appeared that my passion, enthusiasm, and joy shone so brightly that I was seen as a threat.

At the age of thirty-six I discovered I was an empath and naturally drew energy vampires to me. I believe the world is big enough for all of us, but I gave my power away and allowed them to put my fire out.

Frustrated, angry, hurt, annoyed, feeling lost, I took solace and comfort from a harmless substance. Food

"Your body isn't betraying you it's asking for help"
unknown

Food became my best friend, whenever, whatever I felt. Happy, sad, or indifferent. Food does not judge you or talk back to you.

Following the breakup up of my 10-year relationship once again I turned to food.

One day I decided, enough was enough. I did not want my best friend to be a tub of Ben and Jerrys. I planned to call a personal trainer. If he answered I would stop eating the ice cream but if he did not pick up, it was not meant to be, and I would continue this self-destructive path until next time.

Thankfully, the personal trainer picked up and we arranged to meet. I eagerly signed up.

I loved training and before I knew it, I was working out nine to eleven hours a week. I had swapped one addiction for another. One of the trainers made the comment, "You are in here more than me and I work here!".

The gym was a place where I could just switch off. I was super focused on getting to my goal weight. My mindset at the time was that if I lost the weight that my life would be perfect! At that point, I had no social life at all. I chose to work, train, eat, sleep and repeat. After eight months I had lost an impressive five stone. I felt epic, and for once I could shop in any clothes shop and pretty much wear anything and look great.

It was the beginning of a slippery slope. Shopping became my new hobby and I could have given the woman from "Confessions of a Shopaholic "a good run for her money!

I had a body I was proud of, a wardrobe of beautiful clothes, but something was still missing!

Feeling I had now beaten my food demons, I quit the gym and thought, I can do this on my own! Changes within our family, meant my sister had to move back home, which left little room for me. I found a lovely unfurnished flat to rent, a place of my own. I felt excited. The perfectionist came out in me. I knew the look I was going for. Chic and homely, which came with a nice price tag.

I had gone wild and maxed out my flexible friend, and then replaced it with another card, and another. In the end I had quite the collection! I began having sleepless nights. I lived with the constant worry and fear of how I was going to continue to maintain this standard of living. I had a good job, but I did not need to be a rocket scientist to know that my outgoings were far more than my incomings. It did not stop me though. I just kept going and buried my head in the sand.

A few months passed and I knew that at some point, I had to face the music. Finally, I opened the mail and faced up to the chaos! My heart was in my mouth, I fell to the ground, with my mind racing at 100 miles per hour. How did this happen? When did it get so bad?

I thought "OK, breathe and calm down. You just need to come up with a plan of action."

My plan was short sighted and got me further into debt. Whenever my parents visited, they would comment on the numerous shopping bags in my home and I would automatically reassure them.

Little did I know, I was a car crash waiting to happen!

In September 2014 I had to declare bankruptcy as it was my only option. I was totally unprepared for this. I had single-handedly screwed up the next six years of my life. It was not pretty. I was a hot mess. After all the fun, the new clothes, my new body, nothing could prepare me for what was about to happen next. I genuinely thought my life was over, I felt buried alive by debt.

Anxiety does not define you

Shortly after declaring bankruptcy, I took the plunge, moved away, and in with my new partner. We had been dating for a few months. I wanted a fresh start, to draw a line under the mess I had created. Although it would not change the fact of what had happened, or that it would be my shadow for the next six years.

Little did I know that this move would not bring me the happy-ever-after that I envisaged. This would be the catalyst that was going to change my life.

Moving in so quickly with someone was not the greatest plan. The first month together was definitely NOT the fairy tale I had dreamed of.

I was navigating a new relationship, a new town, a new job and trying to settle in. I was excited, nervous, not sleeping, and needed reassurance. This came across as me being needy and clingy.

Then there it was. BOOM! He said that it was best that I move back home as it was not working. He was fed up with me crying myself to sleep, he could not trust me with money, and did not see a future for us. He told me what he was looking for in a woman and I just didn't fit the bill.

After all the expense of moving, I had to ask the bank of mum and dad for a loan to move out. This time I moved into a house where I was a lodger on the other side of town. I tried to see the good points in all of this, but I was incredibly lonely. Being 200 miles from family and friends took its toll. My best friend came to the rescue by coming to stay. I always remember us sitting in the small kitchen, and me moaning about how my life sucked, and her saying to me that it was the greatest thing! I had a great job; the beach was at the bottom of the road and I had no one to answer to. I did not see it that way! A few weeks later, just as I was getting myself on my feet, and even starting to save a little money, my ex phoned, and I picked up. I broke the no contact rule! Bad mistake! Don't do it!

We started seeing each other again, and six months later I was moving back in with him. I thought all our issues were fixed. There was just one rule I had to pay all my moving costs which was fair enough. So just like that I thought everything would turn out just fine and my savings were gone.

Everything was really good for the next three years, every now and then I got itchy feet, the dreamer in me was unsettled, I got bored with everyday life. Getting up, going to work, coming home, dinner and bed. I thought there was more to life!

I always had to be on hand, to dissect the day, whether it was good or bad. I was his emotional crutch. I was on call 24/7, needing to be ready for any situation. It became exhausting, day after day, to have to fill his cup, but not to have the same in return.

I became depleted, emotionally, mentally, and physically. I stopped wanting to go out and do things, stopped doing the chores around the flat. When I spoke to family or friends from back home, they would say I was not my usual self. I was calling my mum twice a day, once in the morning to get up and out to work, and then again at night to decompress from work, so that I had the energy for home.

I was struggling and my mum was too. Eventually she said, "Look you have to find a way, because I can't cope." It was then that I finally went to see my doctor to ask for help. I explained how I felt, and I was diagnosed with severe depression and anxiety. My partner found this too hard to bear, unable to cope with the change in my mental health. The blame was clearly pushed on me, when he said, "I told you it would be difficult moving," There were just to many "I told you so's" being thrown at me. What we had both neglected to see was our relationship was not healthy for either of us. Although we loved each other, it was not enough.

The light bulb moment came when he said his life would be better without me. Quickly followed by him telling me that I was not right in the head, referring to my anxiety and depression. Those were the last words he said to me. In that moment I decided that I would never give my power away nor lose myself in any relationship ever again.

The last time I moved out, my parents had moved heaven and earth to help me, and to learn months later that I had moved back, I had literally ripped their hearts out. My mum said to me that if I ever had to leave again, I was on my own!

My mum is a formidable woman, strong and independent. The morning after, I did not know what to do. I plucked up the courage and called her, explained what had happened and asked for her help. She asked me "How do I know that this time will be any different?" She had a point. I had really hurt both my parents the previous time. I was still relying on them now and had not learned any lessons from the bankruptcy or previous problems in my relationship.

I told her what he had said and said that I would not stand for it. Much to my amazement my mum pointed out that he had said it all before. I did not remember and denied it. But she said "Cheryl he did. It was just that it went over the top of your head because you did not want to hear it"

I said, "Well this time I heard it!" Mum said that she wanted me to be sure I was happy with my decision to leave, and also wanted me to get the relationship out of my system once and for all.

Within days I had found a new place, it was the smallest flat in the world, but it was perfect to me. I had a roof over my head and my own front door. The deposit was paid, but I could not move in for a month. The last month living together was just about bearable, I kept my distance and did things for myself.

After I collected my keys, I moved my stuff in, packing the car the night before and getting to the new place and unloading before work. It was tough and then that Friday morning came, and we said goodbye. I packed the last of my things, dropped off my keys to the agents and drove to my new place. After unloading I look a walk along the beach, and I could finally breathe again.

Healing takes courage, and we all have courage even if we have to dig a little to find it – Tori Amos

The next six months were the best. I had my sanity back. Trust me, that is priceless! Although I had hardly any money, I made the most of my little place. I walked everywhere, made a budget, and stuck to it. There was no need to ask for any more loans from mum and dad. I was repaying the loan from this last move. My room consisted of a camp bed, a bookcase for my collection of books, my TV, a bean bag, a wardrobe, and full-length mirror.

I filled my evenings and weekends with walks along the beach, reading, writing, and learning new skills while healing from my breakup and focusing on all aspects of my health.

I went from just surviving to thriving. I learnt about EFT (Emotional Freedom Technique) and used it as a tool for my mental health and mindset. I found it to be transformational. So much so that when an opportunity arose, I trained as a qualified EFT practitioner. I read some wonderful books and watched TED talks and immersed myself in the self-development world of healing and growth.

Towards the end of my tenancy, I knew that the best thing to do was to return home to be with my family and friends. In some ways it felt like I had failed because it had not all worked out. I felt safe in the knowledge that I had started on a journey of self-discovery to figure out who I was, what I wanted from life and how I was I going to achieve it.

**A strong-minded woman is a different animal
Meryl Streep**

Fortunately, I found a new job immediately and temporarily moved back in with parents.

There was one other thing that I was passionate about. Yoga. I wanted to learn more. A good friend had introduced me to yoga and I really enjoyed it. Then I discovered Dru yoga. I instantly fell in love with how it made me feel. I felt that stillness, inner peace, strength, and connection to spirit throughout my mind and body. I attended weekly classes and within six months I knew that yoga would be a part of my life moving forward. I wanted to share the joy of movement, stillness, inner peace, and strength with other women.

I feel I have come full circle as the last six years and my bankruptcy draw to a close. What I thought would be the ending of me was in truth just the beginning!

What this whole process taught me is that when you hit rock bottom you have two choices. You can either let it crush you, and it will if you allow it to. Or it can be the making of you.

You have really got to dig deep and want to change. You just need to look at all the possibilities open to you.

As they say, as one door closes another one opens. You will never know what is on the other side of the door. Never let fear hold you back, for you have everything within you.

Along the journey, you will outgrow people, sometimes people come into our lives and we go into theirs to hold up mirrors, learn or provide lessons. You will learn this through your own self-awareness.

Never stay where you are being asked to be someone you are not. You cannot fix someone else. You are your own self-healer. People will not change, and we either love and accept them for that, or we love and leave.

How did I change my life? I took and still do, to this day, small steps consistently. I am never afraid to pause to rest and reflect before taking the next step. This is how you create long lasting successful changes. I know this because I because I walked every road, detoured, and derailed before I found my true north, the compass within.

Here are my top six tips to help you start your journey from just surviving to thriving

- mindset is everything;
- you have everything within YOU;
- the most important relationship is the one with YOURSELF;
- set healthy boundaries for yourself and others;
- trust your gut feeling; and
- blaze your own trail.

Cheryl x

Chapter 3 - Natasha Holland

"You are not broken my dear, you are not lost, accepting is believing and believing starts within"
- Natasha Holland

Welcome home for you are not lost.

As I saunter along this undiscovered path, bathing in the forest around me, my senses are awakened at each step and I feel closer to the story I am unveiling for you.

My bare feet grounding me, as the memory of the magic within the damp, mossy forest opens a portal back in time, in my mind.

I have many stories waiting to be written, and many that will be left unwritten, but the story I feel called upon to share in this moment, is a story of self-acceptance, discovery and lessons learnt. I am letting my creativity speak, to invite you to dig deeper within, and encourage you to wake up and welcome the magic of acceptance back into your life.

"A little girl born with a gift
Quirky, creative, a moon child at heart
A day dreamer, a lone believer
Abusing her thoughts and believing their words, she stopped growing into her sparkle
Forming layers and layers and stripping her of self-worth
By rejecting her sparkle, she absorbed vulnerable energy
She fell, fed to the wolves, but when the moon shone bright, the sunrise followed and just like the sun she rose shining her light and warmth
She came back stronger, enlightened with lessons learnt and healed scars"- Natasha Holland

Basking in the misty air around me, I am filling my lungs with colour, light, and energy. Connecting with nature as the soles of my feet submerge into the damp mud, layered with purple heather, decorated artistically with cobwebs and dew drops.

My wildness is awakened, and I am experiencing life on another level where colours look richer and skin feels alive, I can hear and feel things around me like never before, truly living. I look around me and I see the forest coming to life. The singing of the birds, the echo of an owl, a small mouse in the distance carrying its supper.

The nature all around me welcomes me in. We are connected, as one, all together. I feel no fear, nor do they. For I know where I am is where I am meant to be, here in this moment. The consistency of the chalky mud between my toes reminds me of a familiar feeling, put to sleep for many years, but newly awakened once again.

Growing up in a small, remote, village I spent my childhood amongst the trees and in the forest. Where nature and one connect and become whole. Where magic was created and discovered. Bare back pony riding, living without fear of the shadows. I was beautifully FEARLESS in my surroundings, wrapped in the arms of nature, feeling her heartbeat.
The wild child in the woods, flowing in the river, high up in the trees. I did not need to seek clarity for I was clear of thought. The country was the best place for me to be. It allowed the free-spirited child to roam free without expectation. My roots were firm and my intuition alight. I was free and I was living completely in the now, experiencing life at its rawest.

I praise and thank my parents for allowing me to be the child I was, as I appreciate how it would have been challenging otherwise. More so when I was ill.

That took a lot of my mother's time, health, and energy. She dedicated her time to heal me and nursed me when I almost gave up the fight. She taught me a lot about motherhood during those painful years. For that I will be forever grateful. She nursed me back to life, nurturing my soul, body and mind, and she breathed life back into my bones.

Mum says that as a new-born baby I had a gift, able to read people and situations. A psychic gift. I realise now, it is my calling to discover and develop this further to heal, help and guide others. But back then I was simply misunderstood.

I discovered this around between the ages of five and nine. Stuck in the cage called school, I felt ashamed of who l was. It seemed that society had stripped me of my confidence, labelled me, and created layer upon layer of negative belief. I was never supposed to fit into a box, no box was big enough. School was an absolute living hell. Dimming my sparkle. I stopped believing in my inner voice, intuition, and gift. I shut the moon child away and welcomed in societies voice.

"You are not broken my dear, you are not lost, accepting is believing and believing starts within"- Natasha Holland

My belief early on was that I was unteachable. I was split in two. The child at home, roaming in the forest, and the child at school, suffocating and screaming inside. Trapped. The product of a system that was not designed to nurture the wild child.

"Sweet wild child you don't need tamed nor fixed totally free of thought and holding the secrets to true living grounded in soils of growth and magical beyond " - Natasha Holland

A series of events shut me off from learning. I felt like a failure! Punished for my gifted brain. It was not until I was older that I discovered I was dyslexic; another gift that I unveiled and made it my mission to understand.
Welcoming this gift opened a door that I would have never discovered. The door of creativity, learning and belief. It also released me from the expectation that I had to be "perfect!" (A swear word in the holland household).

It was around this time I became a parent, which re-awakened the wildness within, the truth of who I was. My true purpose and calling had become crystal clear to me. I noticed my circle got smaller and I was able to control what energy was around me. This was the start of another journey, a journey of awakening.

"she is not lost, she is still there,
she's your inner voice, your deep intuition,
seeking is believing and believing starts from within,
She is is the barefoot dancing shadow in the distance by the trees,
she is within you and beautifully free,
the touch of the ground beneath her soles fuelled by years of past treasures and gold,
within each woman stands a thousand and holds the key,
The key to unlock the wilderness to be free, so if you seek her, she will answer,
somewhere in between the trees,
so trust yourself and you will see,
the wild women within running free,
for those who ask the questions receive the answers,
the wisdom and the magic, she has the spirit,
she is the soul and all the answers still untold."- Natasha Holland

I was gifted motherhood at the age of 18, shy, an outcast in society. A truly awakening moment. Upgrading my intuition and acknowledging my true calling in life, enabling me to tap into my creativity through photography. Which I used as a coping mechanism throughout my awful childhood illness at the age of 9. It helped me to believe in myself, and to learn, achieve, and conquer! A true blessing.

Motherhood came easy, i just knew what to do! it was truly a magical moment. It triggered in me a primal instinct that instantly challenged my belief system and encouraged me to protect my children from society and its devilish ways. It woke the wild women instinct. I felt alive albeit with bags under my eyes!

Becoming a mother ignited my spiritual journey and gifted me the desire to seek the unknown, to raise my children spiritually and encourage their talents. Inspiring them to step into their magic and to be unique, as this in itself is a superpower! Self-acceptance is the key to living your true purpose and a fulfilled life.

"Free spirited child, promise yourself to never shrink to fit in to other's exceptions
Use your voice and give yourself permission to live your life with your boundaries
You have the right to have your options, view and to say No appreciate your talents and flourish and grow
Take risks and learn
be wild and free" - Natasha Holland

As I am sitting here wondering which way my story is heading, I feel pulled to talk more about the lessons I learnt, and my motherhood journey. But no, I am going to talk about my experience of human life instead. As this is a story I would like you to question.

Life is a gift for those who seek it. I have discovered that many just get by, they think saving or striving for money or status will give them a purpose for life...happiness, fulfilment. Yet at the age of 20 I discovered that this was an error in the system, a fault in this experience we call life. We have taken life for granted; we have overcomplicated living.

Is the answer to strip back and lead a simpler existence? To desire happiness and fulfilment in the present rather than spending our time striving to meet societys expections? To use our talents to heal, and to reap what we sow?

We were born with lungs to breathe, yet many of us don't know how. When did we stop breathing? - Natasha Holland

It is not until we truly accept ourselves that we live our true calling or purpose. Believing starts within, and we have everything within to thrive in our human experience. We are gifted a chance in life to spread love and compassion. To heal ourselves and others around us and learn from our lessons to grow as a better human.

As a woman I felt silenced in this life, felt trapped in the expectations of an ancient ancestral seed, a seed buried deep inside me. But also feeling a sacred duty to break free from that conditioning. To wake the wild woman within me.

Connecting to the elements and experiencing nature is a passion of mine, as well as exploring with creativity, intuition and stepping into my divine feminine energy. I have never felt more alive on this journey! My senses are awakened, and each day brings magic and pure love. Ladies, it is time to remember what it is like to feel alive!
 GO find yourself! Emerge from the chrysalis! It is time to fly!

"I hear the call of the forest pulling me into a magical realm of fantasy and growth as i walk under the canopy of trees I feel at home as feel the heartbeat of the roots below me. Each turning point is a doorway to a new discovery of imagination and creativity. I wander deeper and deeper, but I am not lost, I'm am found." - Natasha Holland

Above I have touched on acceptance. This is a word that has fuelled my life. A word that welcomed the real me without fear, without the need to hide. Welcomed back the inner child who was shut off. This word freed me, gave me the key, held my hand, and showed me the way. Silencing the imposter as it welcomed in truly living and seeing, it slowed me down to appreciate and question. It encouraged me to write this chapter censoring the dyslexic voice inside.

'"Just keep breathing sweet love, this is just a part of your story, a chapter not the whole book, I promise you'll understand when you look back from chapter 20 that this chapter played an important role,
every lesson you learn in this life is an experience, take in the valuable lesson and keep learning and moving forward,
No regrets! Its all part of the plan,
Learn to learn and not hold on,
Find light in the darkest of paths and light the way for others,
Never take a single encounter for granted, never let a conversation pass without meaning, live in the present and evolve each second,
Each moment in your path is there for you…. question and never lose your curiosity" - Natasha Holland

Self-Acceptance

So, what does this phrase mean and why is it so powerful? Or you may be thinking, how the hell can a word or a phrase really change your way of thinking?

This is what I have learnt on my journey of self-love and acceptance.

To answer the question, self-acceptance is one hundred percent accepting the person you are. Your personality, talents, looks, and even your current life situation, as well as your past. It is about accepting your lessons, choosing growth, and accepting future lessons. It is about accepting every side of you and looking at yourself with love, kindness, strength, and compassion.

I truly believe that self-acceptance is the key to fulfilment, happiness, self-love, and positivity. A key to valuing your dreams and aspirations, for loving the journey you are on and the person you are. Letting go of the imposters and negative talk and totally trusting the outcome of your decisions. You can do anything you put your mind to, and you have no limitations! You are fearless when you create! And your creativity flows and welcomes in new opportunities.
If you accept yourself, you will find others around you accept you too, and it will give them permission to do the same. When you raise your frequency and send your vibrations out to the universe you will attract back what you desire. You will step into your own calling with ease and flow and no negative belief system will hold you back.

Its ok to have crap days. Days where you feel down and not up to scratch. That is normal and oh so very human. Emotions are part of human life and are essential for us to exist and express.

Acknowledgment and curiosity about your emotions will unveil the message for you. We listen to others, but can you imagine if you actually started listening to yourself? You would feel loved, honoured, and heard.

"I have come to fully accept myself and the life I am in and I the power within to do anything I wish, If I'm not happy I give myself permission to change and grow." - Natasha Holland

Self-acceptance is believing in your power and strength, celebrating each other for who we are, our purpose, our divine magic. Its refusing to be crushed, censored, or tamed! It encourages us to take risks, trust our intuitions and the universe! We are all connected as one. We breathe out our thoughts and beliefs into the universe, so raise your vibrations and frequency by accepting all of yourself for who you are, breathing out love and compassion.

Thank you very much for reading this passage to self-acceptance and discovery. Life is a journey and not a destination. Welcome back for you are not lost… Acceptance is believing and believing starts within.

Love and Light
Natasha Holland
x x x

Chapter 4 - L N Sheffield

Copyright The Inner Feminine Collective 2020

Our deepest fear is not that we are inadequate. Our deepest fear is that we are powerful beyond measure.
It is our light, not our darkness that most frightens us.
We ask ourselves, Who am I to be brilliant, gorgeous, talented, fabulous? Actually, who are you not to be?
You are a child of God. Your playing small does not serve the world.
There is nothing enlightened about shrinking so that other people won't feel insecure around you.
We are all meant to shine, as children do.
We were born to make manifest the glory of God that is within us.
It's not just in some of us; it's in everyone.
And as we let our own light shine, we unconsciously give other people permission to do the same.
As we are liberated from our own fear, our presence automatically liberates others.

~ Marianne Williamson

I have drunk all my life.

Ever since I was 15 and first tasted Hooch. My god! Do you remember that drink? It was like alcoholic lemonade, sweet and fizzy. And it was new and all the rage back then. Then my friend, who was a couple of years older, told me to try cider. I never looked back. It was my drink for the next 20 odd years! Well my main drink anyway. It was cheap, tasted nice with some blackcurrant in it, to sweeten it, and of course it gave me that floaty, relaxed feeling after a few. I loved that feeling so much, I was so addicted! I never wanted it to go away. I usually kept drinking until I passed out. I wanted to keep hold of the feeling, but it always got out of hand.

I used to go out clubbing a lot when I was younger and always suffered with such bad hangovers in those days. I would develop a migraine and be sick 4-8 times during the day. I would stay in bed until at least 5pm and could not stomach a thing to eat, until the sickness had passed. You would think I would have learned, but no. All I needed was a day or two to get over it and I was back on it again. Well it was only £2.49 for a pack of 4 cans of cider from the corner shop in those days. It was hardly breaking the bank. But at the weekends I would easily spend £40+ on a night out with friends.

As time passed, I did not go clubbing so much. My friends began relationships, started making families, settling down. So, I found new friends and went to the pub most nights after work. Especially with my best friend at the time. I was 18. She was about 16 years older than me, but such a fun person to be around. We worked together. And every night we would go to the pub for a couple, and then round to her place or mine and drink cans all night. Sometimes we skipped the pub and went straight to one of our homes to drink.

She would have her lager and I would have my cider & black. It felt relaxing and fun when we drank. And because I was relaxed, I could share what was on my mind. There was no way I was brave enough to speak my mind without the aid of booze! That was why I drank. It made me brave. I wanted to be cool like my friend, keep up with her. Drinking made that possible.

Somehow, we managed to turn up to work each day, no matter how rough we felt. She was the manager and I was the assistant manager. We took it in turns to sit in the office and close the door if we needed to. But we still managed to make it back over to the pub later. I would force myself to have a "hair of the dog" because after one went down ok it made me feel better. And then the fuzziness kicked back in.

Fast forward – Its 2020 and I am 39 this year.

I first began to question my drinking back in 2012. I was in my first serious relationship and I knew my drinking was affecting it. She was an amazing woman. I did not want to ruin things. We had been together around 2 or 3 years, but when I drank, I wasn't very nice to her - verbally. It is a long time ago now and I can't remember all the details. But looking back, I know I was angry with myself and at the world and when I got drunk, she took the brunt of it. It was not nice for her, and I did not want to be that person.

I began talking to my auntie. We spoke every week and I had no need to tell her any of my perceived "problems". We just spoke about what created our experience. The role that thought played in our lives. We explored the truth of who we are at our core. It did not seem like we were directly addressing my issues, but life got a whole lot better over the next few years. Something shifted in me and resonated with what I was hearing and learning about my thoughts and feelings. About how our experience is created.

I had seen my auntie Deb change so much. She had left a 20-year abusive relationship and had come so far. I was so inspired by her. I wanted to give up alcohol altogether, but there was no way that was going to happen. I decided that I could learn to drink "normally" and not be so dependent on booze. And I wanted to stop being so abusive to my partner when I had drink inside me. It was the best I could hope for and I could not allow myself to see any further than that. I was not ready to face the whole of my life without alcohol FOREVER. It was way too scary.

I reduced my alcohol intake significantly. But I did not quit altogether. There were still a lot of situations and events that I could not face without alcohol. The best thing was that I did start to feel calmer and nicer inside myself, and even when I did drink, I wasn't nasty to my partner like I used to be. It was a huge step forward.

My relationship with my partner improved. For the next couple of years our relationship changed for the better. We grew closer and I was a lot nicer to her. My drinking did not stop completely, but for a while I drank less often.

But sadly, we hit some problems and split up. I think the main reason was that I was still learning and growing, and it felt like we were on different paths. I was discovering so much from Deb and our chats. Things that held me back before were dropping away and I was becoming more "me".

When we split up it was hard. We had a mortgage and a lot of things to sort out. I did not deal with it very well and I guess this is when I really began to slip back into my old drinking habits. I remember one evening getting pretty drunk and even though we were apart we still had contact because we were sorting out the house. I sent her some really nasty messages. I was not a very happy person. The anger took over and came out again. I felt so guilty the next morning. She did not deserve that.

Back A Bit - December 2019

My partner and I had been split for well over 3 years. I had had plenty of dates and a few short relationships since then. My sister Bec and I had finally moved to Devon in May 2018 to work and live with my auntie, sharing this understanding of the mind, and helping others.

By this time, my drinking was completely out of control again. I was drinking 4 or 5 nights a week. Easily consuming at least one bottle of wine each time. I was kidding myself it was ok because I wasn't hurting anyone. I wasn't nasty when I drank now. What harm was it doing?

I could feel that the other people in our house thought I drank too much and too often. But they loved me, and I knew they would not judge me. They knew I had to see it for myself.

I was in a relationship again. We had only been together around 4 months, but I was starting to feel a bit panicky and not normal about our sex life. My heavy drinking continued.

I was scared to admit it to anyone but one day I bravely reached out and told my sister that I struggled having sex without the aid of my trusty old friend wine holding my hand all evening. When I had a few, or a bottle, I felt more relaxed and confident. When I was drunk there was no problem. But when it came to sober sex, I did what I could to avoid it. I had created this huge story in my mind that I was not confident enough without drinking. That I needed it to relax me. That without it I could not bring myself to do it.

I didn't want this to be an issue in my relationship. Putting it out there and talking to my sister made me feel a little better. I began to explain that it was not just the sex stuff, there were many other reasons that I drank too much.

Speaking with Bec, I realised that I had opened a whole can of worms. But I felt HUGE relief at being open and honest. Just saying it out loud helped so much.

There were many things that I convinced myself I could not do without drinking. They looked so solid to me.

I could not go to a party or a wedding or any other kind of night out without getting drunk. No way Jose!

I started exploring these ideas in my head. I didn't say any more to Bec that day. But I started questioning. Started looking at everything that I told myself was impossible if I was sober.

What if I could? I asked myself.

I did say to Bec that "I can see that I am getting curious about my relationship with alcohol, but I can see that I don't need to do anything else. It's not all on me."

In that moment I really saw that. There was a recognition, an awareness. I had begun to realise that I wanted my relationship to alcohol to change.

I had wanted things to change before but it always looked too hard. Because I thought it was all down to me. It was easier not to bother. When things look hard, we make excuses. Admitting it to myself made a massive difference. It was progress.

I know that the universe has my back. I am aware that this can sound a little woo-woo so don't take my word for it. Try it for yourself. In whatever way that works for you. Some people find praying or asking God for help works. For me? Well I just kept questioning things and trying stuff - exploring.

The answer here is knowing, and I mean really knowing deep within your gut, that there is a bigger force at work. It has our back and is working in our favour. It hears what we genuinely desire and it conspires to help us. We can trust in life.

After that many things started happening. To my mind it was the universe sending things my way to help me with what I had asked for.

For instance. In my writing practice, shared with my mentor each week, I wrote a little bit about how I was so under-confident in the bedroom without wine to relax me. I felt safe and ok to talk it through with her. She knew now, so I had nothing to hide. In fact, she said to me "I am sure you are not alone in these feelings. So many people will relate to this you know."

This gave me the confidence to share with others. I began telling more and more people my "sex and alcohol" story and suddenly it didn't seem all that scary anymore. Many people came back to me and opened up with their own versions of that story.

I began to see that I was not weird, abnormal, or not good enough. And it was ok to speak out loud about my biggest fears and darkest secrets. In fact, my honesty helped me, and helped others, feel safe and able to share things.

The ironic thing was, in the midst of all of this, my relationship with my partner broke down. How I found the strength to stop drinking whilst going through a very unpleasant break-up I have no idea. But now I know. I reckon it was that trusty old universe. It was more dependable than my old friend wine, that was for sure.

While trying to sort things out with my partner I made a brave decision. I decided to take the plunge and embark on my 30-day alcohol experiment.

FUCK IT! I thought, what have I got to lose?

I wanted to change. I wanted to drink like a normal person. I wanted to be able to go out and have a couple of glasses of wine and just be sociable. I was sick of feeling so tired and off key.

You know the biggest thing I wanted to do?

I wanted to feel things naturally. I wanted to embrace all of my feelings. I did not want to be scared of feeling anxious or nervous or any of the other stuff that came up. I wanted to let those feelings be there and be ok with them.

Drinking wine numbed them. I felt like I was cheating myself from feeling ALL the feelings.

Finally, I was ready!

Little did I know I was going to enjoy being sober so much, that I could see myself not drinking again. Who knows I may do! I started by wanting to get a grip on my relationship with alcohol, but I knew that for any lasting change I needed to start by cutting it out completely.

Never for one moment did I think I would not have any desire to drink again.

7 Months On - Still Alcohol Free

Life feels pretty normal now. I rarely think about drinking. I have changed so much over the last 7 months. I can see it and feel it and other people comment too.

The main change is how confident I feel in myself on a day to day basis. I rarely get days when I am depressed now. I have so much more natural energy.

I genuinely love life!

Now I no longer need wine holding my hand, there is nothing stopping me from being me. Lucy.

As I write this my friend has just gone home after a few days visiting with me. We were lucky to have the most gorgeous weather. We went out for a meal on two of the evenings, and I admit I struggled a bit. My friend had a glass of wine with her dinner and I felt envious. I really felt the urge to have something cold and refreshing sitting in the sunshine.

But what I was clear on, was that I did not want to get drunk. I have no desire for that fuzzy feeling anymore. In fact, I cannot think of anything worse. I love feeling clear headed. I love the natural high of life. But I acknowledge that I did want to feel normal and be able to choose to have just one drink with my dinner.

I chose a non-alcoholic ginger beer and felt really proud of myself for not giving into it.

I am interested in seeing what happens next, whether those feelings come up for me again. I am nervous that I will slip back into my old drinking habits. But, having such a long time off the drink, with my head so clear, seeing how amazing it is on this side of things, I don't think I need to worry too much, or take it too seriously.

My ultimate dream and goal was to be able to drink "normally". To go out for dinner with people and have a wine or two and be satisfied with that.

Now I see it like this - I do not want to be stuck in a mindset where I feel that I cannot do something. Having had the time to explore how it feels to be alcohol free, I want to be able to drink on occasion if I wish to. But by granting myself that permission, I am fairly sure that I will choose not to.

When we let ourselves off the hook and allow ourselves to do things, we will do more of what we genuinely want, in line with what makes sense to us.

I am thoroughly enjoying my life now. For the first time I am doing what I love each day and it comes from my soul. I have become an abstract artist over the last five months, and I have an urge to inspire other women to follow their dreams and creativity. Letting go of the alcohol and the fear, I have allowed creativity to flow through me. I now make a living from selling my artwork, and I have also just published my first children's book.

If you have enjoyed reading this and would like to know where the next part of my journey takes me, please get in touch!

I love to connect with people and help them realise their potential. My wish is that this story has inspired you. Please reach out if there is any way I can help you to see the beauty of life again, or if you want to hear the long version!

Chapter 5 - Helen Bartram

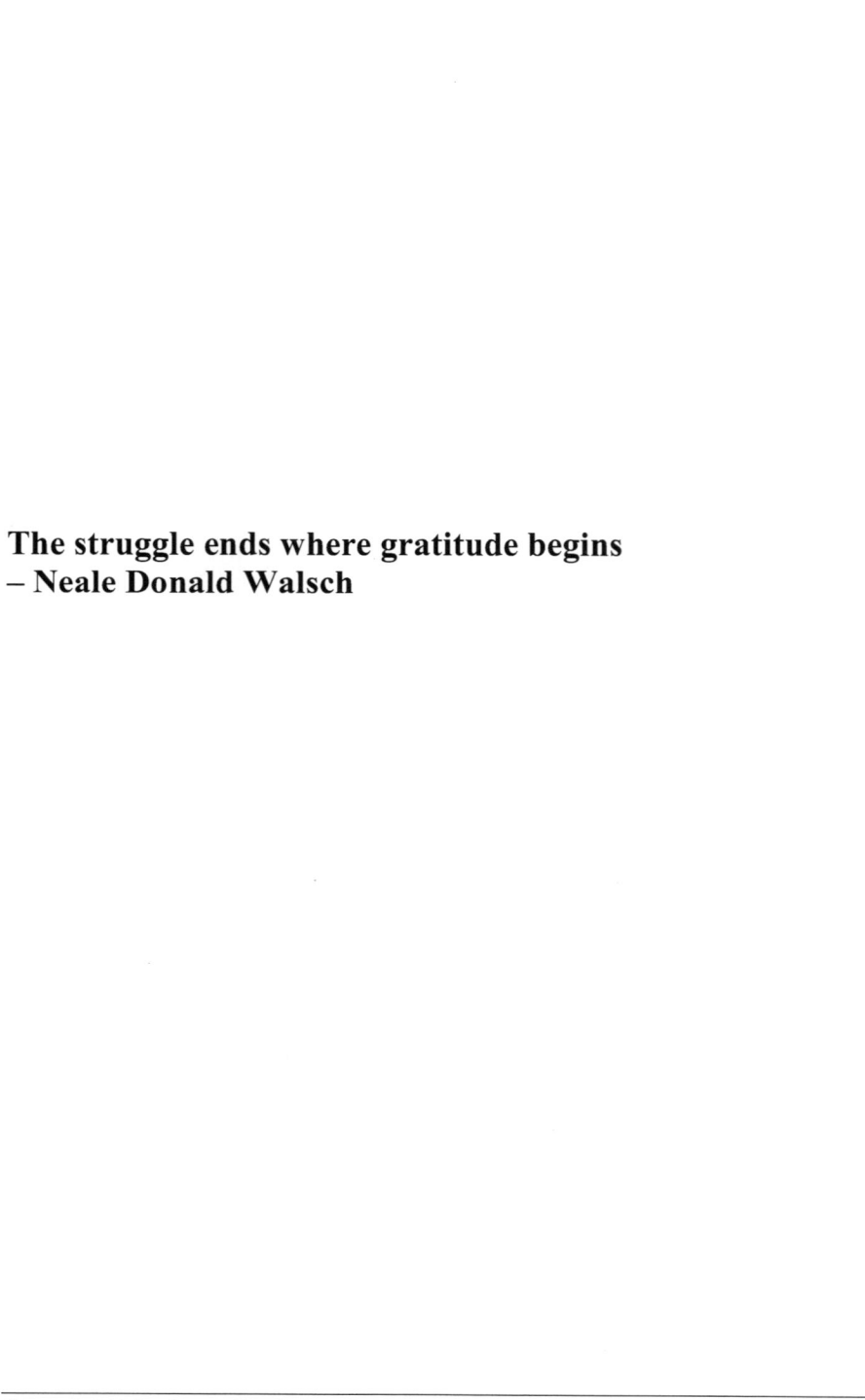

The struggle ends where gratitude begins
– Neale Donald Walsch

The Year that changed everything.

As I sit here and write this for you, I want you to understand I am sharing something I have never shared with anyone in such detail before. It would have been easier to have printed a naked picture of myself and placed it right here on this page for the world to see! I would have felt less exposed.

This is for you – If you take one piece of inspiration or valuable information from my story, then exposing my vulnerability has been worthwhile.

I write this sitting on a fluffy mustard coloured blanket, with the sun shining down on me and my heart filled with gratitude. Today, like every other day I welcome happiness, I choose to listen to my heart, and I accept that I am enough.

It has not always been this way. If you had been with me on 9th February 2018 at 8.30pm you would have found me in a heap on a cold, grey, laminate floor. My heart was shattered into a million pieces and I was silently sobbing into my hands afraid that any noise would wake the children who were fast asleep upstairs. What I really wanted to do was wail...loudly. Scream and shout! But at that point I did not have the energy for that.

My life was a fucking mess.

Moments prior to this he had left. The heavy, white door literally slammed behind him, and I had collapsed in a heap on the floor. I am not sure how I had managed to keep the strength in my legs until this point.

Years of carrying everyone else's shit around with me finally overwhelmed me – and BANG I was on the floor. As I looked up at the back of the door where the keys were still swinging, a small part of me wanted to chase after him. Tell him to come back; that I loved him, and we could make this work. The other half of me wanted to run somewhere very far away and never look back.

In that moment I had a flash back to the last time I experienced this urge to run. About 4 years prior to this, I had been diagnosed with a missed miscarriage. I was sitting in a side room in the hospital and I remember thinking that perhaps I could just run away from all of this, and then everything would be okay.

Have you ever had a time in your life where you just wanted to run and hide, convinced that everything you were running away from would magically resolve? Wouldn't that be nice?

But lying on that cold laminate floor I knew that that was bullshit. We cannot run away from our problems. We always take them with us. Eventually we must face them. I reminded myself how I overcame the pain of the miscarriage and that life continued even though I felt broken.

I am sure there have been times in your life when you have overcome something so huge that you felt that it would defeat you. These moments serve to remind us of our resilience, strength, persistence, and courage. All the resources we use to help us through life's challenges.

But at that moment, lying on the cold floor, my heart was breaking. Not just for me, but for those beautiful souls sleeping upstairs. I watched as we told them that Daddy was going to be moving out for a while, and I saw their world collapse as my heart did. "How much more shit can one family take?" I asked myself.

Being a parent is the most rewarding job, but also challenging. So many questions to answer; Am I doing the right thing? Am I protecting them enough? Am I good enough?

I always believed in being as transparent as possible as a parent. I did not want my children growing up seeing me as a robot, scared of facing challenges or experiencing emotions. The universe had been sending me challenge after challenge. In fact, 2018 felt like one long challenge!

The following morning, I got up early and did what I do best. I carried on. While there was still air in my lungs, I would carry on. I would not give up.

For me, "carrying on" served as a distraction. Distracting me from dealing with what was really going on around me. From the shit showing up in my life, that had been building up for years. I threw myself into being a good mum, a good friend. Being there for every man and his dog! But in doing so I lost sight of myself. The moment my husband walked out the door the penny dropped. I saw that I had lost my identity.

This morning after was no different to any other morning. I was there waiting to greet the children as they woke, I got them ready for school and then I headed into university. Just 4 months before I had started a 3-year psychology and counselling degree. I vividly remember during enrolment week, one my friends saying, "they say married people who study psychology are twice as likely to end up getting a divorce".

I am not sure where this statistic came from, but I remember rolling my eyes and thinking 'yeh, right'. Was this the psychology student curse? I had quit what my grandma described as a ''decent job'' working in finance to study for this degree after deciding to go with my gut instinct and knowing that I had more to give to the world. Looking back now, it is laughable! How could I give anything to the world when I was already spread thinner than thin?

Arriving at university, I checked in with 'the girls' at the local coffee shop. I told them that my husband had moved out, and I could feel their pity. All eyes on me and my life.

I was longing for a fairy godmother to swoop in and sort all this shit out. To wave her magic wand and make everything grand! I grew up watching Disney movies where everyone lived happily ever after. In reality, the only person who could save me and my life from this train wreck was me. I skipped my first lecture and found a quiet corner in the library of the university. I took out a note pad and I brain dumped all the shit that was flying round in my head. I looked at all the things that were weighing me down and had been, for as long as I could remember. I realised, there in that moment, that most of the things that had been having a negative effect on me and my life were out of my control.

My mother-in-law had been terminally ill for eight years. That had brought painful challenges into our lives. Also, my grandma was diagnosed with terminal cancer shortly after I started University. Then, just two weeks prior to this crisis, my mum had been diagnosed with breast cancer.

In addition, my daughter's epilepsy, a lack of communication and 'us' time in my marriage; a lack of self-care, and me running around trying to fix everyone else's problems; it all came with a heavy price. I had I lost sight of myself.

Juggling one thing after another, fighting fires, rescuing others and desperately trying to find time for making memories with loved ones while they were still here; I had lost touch with 'normal' life and was existing on some kind of intense emotional rollercoaster.

I felt anxious all the time. I worried to excess, there were very few moments in the day where I felt at peace with nothing concerning me. And even in those rare moments I would be mentally searching for something else that I should be worrying about. Worrying had become my comfort zone. I was the Queen of Distraction and avoided time alone as it was not a pleasurable experience.

Maybe you can relate to some of this. Perhaps you have been, or are the go-to person, who helps solve everyone else's problems. While ignoring your own. Running yourself into the ground helping other people stay afloat. But when you have a problem or are struggling with a challenge – it seems there is no one around to pick up the pieces.

Well that is how I felt right there in that moment. When we appear to be 'strong' in the world, everyone assumes that we have it all together and that we can handle whatever shit gets thrown our way. We become so used to being the helper that when we need help, we have no idea how to ask for it.

There were people around me who could, and would, help me rebuild my life – it was just that I was too afraid to ask.

I kept asking myself how had I ignored my exhaustion and my gut feelings for so long? I felt drained every single day. I had disconnected myself from those closest to me. I ignored my own feelings and I was disassociating myself from all the little pockets of trauma bubbling away in every corner.

I wore a mask every day. Hiding behind a smile and presenting some positive cheesy quote to the world because I felt that was who the world needed me to be. There was so much pressure to be everything to everyone. Pressure I had willingly invited into my life. Feeling that I had no choice but to carry on 'playing' my chosen role in the world.

What bullshit! I know now that we always have a choice. It was time. To burn the mask and drop all the jigsaw pieces of my life onto the floor. Then I could start rebuilding ME, one piece at a time.

Where do you begin when you no long know who you are? I was wearing many different hats, one for each of the roles I had been carrying. But how did I reconnect with myself? I was avoiding dealing with all the pain and sadness I was experiencing. What I discovered was that we can let our pain, problems and challenges define us OR we can choose to RISE like a phoenix from the ashes!

We are not born to be defeated. No matter what life throws our way, we can change or overcome every situation with a little acceptance, kindness, and belief. Trust me when I say, I get it. It does not always seem possible. If you are knee deep in a shitty situation, feeling lost or stuck; you cannot see the light at the end of the tunnel. Believe me I have been there.

One of the biggest lessons I have learned is to accept that every situation and circumstance is temporary. Whether you are experiencing an amazing feeling, or going through something terrible, the worst experience in the world, it will always pass. It is always temporary. That is why it is super important for us to live in the moment. Soak up all the good stuff when amazing things happen. But when we are experiencing dark times, the lonely, shitty moments where it feels like things will always feel that shitty. Know that '' This too shall pass ''.

The weeks following my insight were very, very challenging. With all the jigsaw pieces of my life spread out on the floor, I felt like a rag doll being pulled through life with no meaning or purpose other than to survive. I allowed myself to be influenced by everyone I met. I was on that emotional rollercoaster and I had no trust in my own judgement. I began putting more weight onto other people's words whether they were offering sympathy, advice, a kick up the arse, or inspiration. But in doing so I found I was losing myself even more.

I remember a conversation with my mum one day as I left university. She had been booked in for a mastectomy. The doctor was sure this would remove any cancer cells and she would be all clear. She was upbeat and positive and saying how lucky she was that it was curable.

For a moment I paused and thought about some of the people I held closest in my heart. People who despite their own pains and challenges they faced in life taught me so much about myself and the world:

My mother-in-law who had fought her cancer battle for almost 8 years now, after being told she was likely to survive 12-18 months after diagnosis. She was truly inspirational, she loved watching her grandchildren grow up, and there was no way she was giving up the fight until she was ready.

My grandma, a tough cookie who grew softer in her later years. A woman who knew what she wanted and was not afraid to get it. She never had it 'easy' in life but one thing I had learnt from her was that happiness is always an option! Even when we face tough challenges, we can still live a fulfilled meaningful life.

My auntie, someone who would always have words of wisdom to offer or simply just hold a space for me to release. She never judges, she always stays true to herself and genuinely loved seeing people being happy and doing well for themselves in life.

Then, my own mum. A woman who had moments before told me how lucky she was that her cancer diagnosis was not terminal. I was surrounded by pretty awesome and inspirational women. It was time to rediscover my own awesomeness.

I would love to tell you that I went on some self-discovery journey, put all the jigsaw pieces back together and went on to live a life of happy ever afters. But it was not as easy as all that. Holding a mirror up to see who I was, discovering who I no longer wanted to be, and who I had become was fucking difficult. I knew I had to do it, in order to discover what I wanted for my future. But initially I could not even look in the mirror without feeling sick. I did not feel good enough, worthy, pretty enough.

I barely recognised myself, and sometimes impatience would get the better of me. I would get frustrated and angry at myself for not immediately knowing the answers to my own questions. For not knowing what direction I wanted to head in, and for years and years of doing what others and society expected me to do.

Thing did start to shift, and I knew that I was making progress, but the challenges continued to come. Clashes within friendship circles, health scares, loss, and grief. But it taught me that there are always going to be challenges. I was learning to feel happiness and have peaceful moments whatever life threw at me.

It was difficult. There were two young children looking to me to steer their ship, when I felt like my ship was sinking. I learnt a huge lesson in this period. I had got so comfortable with always having my foot on the gas in fourth gear, but I began to see that it is perfectly ok to drop a gear, or two. It's even fucking ok to take the car out of gear and just freaking cruise for a little while! Just navigate each moment as it comes and then move onto the next. It is okay to not have it all planned out.

I started setting aside time every day to focus on things I felt grateful for, looking at myself in the mirror and reconnecting to my values and what was important to me. I took the time to examine each piece of the jigsaw puzzle that under a microscope and evaluate whether it belonged in my life anymore. Gradually the jigsaw puzzle became a complete picture, one piece at a time.

Looking back now, sitting here in the glorious sunshine, I can truly be grateful for each of the challenges and shitty times I have experienced in my life. I can see that I did my very best with each situation, given the information and knowledge that I had at that time.

By reconnecting with myself and learning to listen to my gut, I have started to take care of myself. And that means that I can take care of others. Having learned that every emotion or situation is temporary, I can honestly say that I live each day with my heart filled with love and gratitude. Some days are still shit, some days are exceptionally spectacular, but that's life and I've learned to appreciate every step of my journey, enjoy the small things, be present and know that Inner Peace begins With a Grateful Heart.

Chapter 6 - Hazel Carter

"Life isn't about waiting for the storm to pass...It's about learning to dance in the rain."

- Vivian Greene

Two years ago, I thought I had resolved my problems. It was January, the beginning of a new year, a fresh start. I had big plans for my life. I had quit the secure civil service job I loved, to become a carer for my children and run a self-employed business doing something that would fit around our lives. The previous three years, since my children were born, had been the most challenging of my life so far.

Life has always been turbulent for me and if asked, I would say "my life is one shit show rolling into the next". I believed that after everything I had been through I was resilient, I could handle anything.

My expectations of life were fairly low. Happiness seemed to be out of my reach. I was doing alright and that was enough. If I could keep on managing, then everything would be fine.

Then I met someone, and I thought maybe, just maybe the shit show was ending; he seemed to be a perfect match. Little did I know. I had known him for a while before we got together. We had a lot in common, similar outlooks on life, shared interests, and seemed to be at a similar point in our lives. Both of us were ready to settle down and have children.

Things moved quickly and after a relatively short time I became pregnant and we moved in together. We were starting a new life together. New home, child on the way, both in good jobs. Life was looking good. The dream everyone wants.

Early in the relationship there were a few 'red flags' but I dismissed them. After all that would not happen to me, would it? I knew the signs, I was a strong independent woman, and I had training in helping people who had gone through domestic abuse situations. I was not one of those people. But the truth is it can happen to anyone.

At the twelve-week scan, two days after moving into our new home, we found out we were having twins and with that came a whole raft of additional information and risks.

My "perfect match" became more erratic, more aggressive, and dismissive of me and our unborn children. I put his behaviour down to the stress of pregnancy, the additional scans, and the possible risks of having twins that we had been warned about.

I told myself everything would be fine once they were born, wouldn't it? But it wasn't.

Once the twins were born, the abuse escalated way beyond levels that I would ever have thought that I would accept. It was a slow escalation. It happened under the radar.

I realised that I needed to work out what was best for the children. I was barely sleeping, and I was mentally, physically, and emotionally exhausted. I was diagnosed with severe sleep deprivation. I felt incapable of looking after the children on my own. I could not leave him, and I could not tell anyone. I was ashamed that I had become one of 'those women'. I was trapped.

This went on for over a year. Then something happened. The abuse didn't change, but his false accusations went a step too far. I found myself sitting in the back of a police van. I woke up. I'd had enough. The relationship ended; he moved out; I was alone with the children.

I had very little family support, no close friends and two small children. One of my boys has behavioural challenges, and the other has many health problems and severe developmental issues. He is unable to walk, non-verbal, issues with food, with breathing, and repeated chest infections, with his feet and had absence seizure epilepsy. The list goes on. I was told by health professionals that he was one of the children with the most severe additional needs in the borough.

In addition, I had a house to upkeep and a stressful job. Managing became the order of the day. Endless medical appointments, therapies, and assessments. Dealing with the unique needs of my two very young children. Working extra hours at home most nights. Dealing with the mental strain associated with my children's father. Surviving day to day, with little or no sleep.

On top of what felt like never-ending, unmanageable housework in a house that required significant renovation. Swamped by the mountain of tasks that presented each and every day. Repeating to myself over and over 'I can do this', 'I can do this'. And I did for nearly two years.

But the toll on me and my relationship with my children, and my ability to be the mother I wanted to be was substantial. I was clinging on by my fingertips; both my physical and mental health had deteriorated significantly.

Then there was a major change at work. Meaning restructure and re-training. I had no capacity to take this on. I had no choice. I had to leave my job or risk my physical or mental health reaching breaking point.

I told everyone about the big plans I had for all my spare time now I was not working. I would start my own business. I would be on top of the housework. The house would be re-decorated, and I would have no issues attending the numerous health appointments for my children.

I was so wrong. I think I had been surviving on pure adrenaline because I crashed hard. Everything was an effort; I was exhausted physically and mentally. I did not know where to start, or how to make anything better. I was drowning. I was miserable and in a lot of physical pain. I knew there had to be more; life had to be better.

I had never sought help from anyone. I was the person that people came to for help and advice. But I had to accept that it was time to ask for help.

I started attending carers groups and joining online communities. It seemed a good place to start; these people would understand. I struggled; I didn't feel I belonged. I sat quietly, and that is not my style! I was lonely and exasperated with my situation. But I kept trying.

I started a course for carers about children's behaviour, it was the same people each week and I began to open up, but still did not see myself as one of 'those parents', a parent whose life was all about caring for the child with additional needs, to the exclusion of everything else. I wanted more for me and my boys.

I started a business, upcycling furniture. It was difficult. I was passionate but scared and struggled to find the time and energy to do the work needed to make it successful. I joined business groups and a new networking group for mums. It was friendlier than other groups I'd been involved with. Then I found an associated local group with women from the north east of England. I felt on the same wavelength as many of these women. I felt drawn to them. A new experience in a business group.

These women were strong, passionate, capable, and free. I did not feel I could ever be like that. Life was too hard, too exhausting, and I was just surviving, just managing to get through each day. I was trying. I had sought help with my life as a carer, and with running a business, but still felt like I was drowning.

Each morning in the early hours I was woken for the day by one or both of my boys screaming, the kind of screaming that seeps deep inside your brain, knowing most of the time you won't be able to find a reason, or a solution, failing day after day to find a way to help.

I would drag my exhausted, aching body out of bed. Every day I would think "here we go again"! I would work through the list of things that might help today. Some days the screaming carried on for hours. It was a good day if I found a resolution quickly. I kept telling myself 'just keep going'.

When you are at rock bottom it is the small things that help. For me it was finding a moment to drink a cool glass of water from the tap. Getting to that point each morning, feeling the cool water on my lips was such a relief. It usually meant that both boys were settled and calm, for now at least.

Every day was an endless round of tears and meltdowns, stress and anxiety, medication and therapies, pain, and discomfort, worries and hopes. Bedtime brought more stress, more tears, more screaming, more medication, and fear for what the night would bring. They did not sleep through the night.

I lived with an underlying, nagging fear that this was how the rest of our lives would be. Life had thrown so many challenges my way. I was resilient, strong, independent, intelligent and I had got this far. Why did it have to be so hard?

I wanted more; a better life for me and my boys. But I could not see a way out of the hole we were in.

I am not sure exactly when things began to change. It was a slow process, influenced by several people. Women in the business group, friends I made through mum's groups, the local carer's groups. Over six months the fog began to clear, advice started to make sense, and everything settled.

The first step towards a happier life was a small thing, but massive to me. It was about acceptance. Of myself, who I was. Of my boys and their needs. I accepted that my family was only ever going to provide limited support. That the boy's dad would never step up. Life was always going to be a challenge. I accepted that there were things I could not control.

There was no miracle fix.

It was not easy to say that I accepted all this. But I was wasting so much energy trying to change things that were beyond my control. This was a turning point for me in my journey.

I now found I had time, and the energy to look at the things I could change. The things I *could* do to make our lives happier. This change in my mindset helped me get a clearer picture of the challenges and difficulties we faced.

Over the next few months, I realised that I needed to take better care of myself. Up until now, my self-care consisted of those precious glasses of water and copious amounts of good coffee. My treat was making myself an Americano. It felt ridiculously extravagant.

I used to see 'self-care Sunday' posts in mum's online groups. Frankly, I found this idea hilarious! Doing something for myself, on a Sunday, with two children in the house? Who has time for sumptuous baths, massages, getting their nails done and all that jazz, with children?

It took me a while to realise that pampering was one kind of self-care. But it is about so much more. As they say, "You cannot pour from an empty cup". My 'cup' was almost completely empty. I started doing some really small things for myself. Giving myself a five-minute-mini-manicure. Buying some nice chocolate. Sitting in the car for an extra few minutes to listen to a song. Small things to look forward to that made me feel good. I still did not believe I could do much more. But it was a start.

It was now a whole year since I had left my job. But I felt that very little had changed. Life was calmer; I was a bit more relaxed, more settled. Mentally I had come a long way from the dark months at the start of the year. But the house was still a mess, business was a struggle both physically and mentally, and the mountain of housework was still present.

My physical health was becoming more of an issue as my boys got older, bigger, and heavier to carry and I struggled to play physical games with them. But I was starting to get a glimpse of myself and my future, a life of adventure and happiness.

I was about to turn forty. What better time to make a new start, draw a line in the sand and make it count for me and my boys. I made a list of forty things to do in my fortieth year. Some small, some massive challenges. I like a list and ticking them off was an incentive. I was going to say yes to new things and see where that took me.

Top of my list was the Great North Run! The biggest half marathon in the country. Well if I was going to do something, I might as well go big. I was unfit, overweight, every bit of my body ached constantly, and I wasn't sure if my back or pelvis worked properly anymore. For fifteen years I had been saying I was going to do this run. It was now or never. I secured a charity place with the organisation which provided weekly therapy for my son. Seeing it as a huge commitment and a chance to repay some of the amazing help and support we had received.

But it was a massive challenge. I couldn't risk making my physical health worse, so I had to do it right. I started a program of treatments and self-care so that I could take part. I rarely spent money on myself; I could not remember the last time I had even bought any clothes. But first things first. A sports massage to sort out my aches and pains. At my first appointment, the therapist made tutting noises and there were sharp intakes of breath. Her assessment was that my back was one of the stiffest, most knotted, that she had ever seen. She recommended an osteopath as my pelvis was out of line.

The osteopath compared my back to that of a ninety-year-old and told me not to run at all until she said so. I was disheartened, but soon realised it was a good thing. If I had carried on trying to manage the pain, I could have ended up in a much worse state and would have struggled even more with the boys.

Years and years of me neglecting my body had led to these problems. The treatments became a regular feature in my life. It was very strange, focusing on me. Once I was given the green light, I started training. I completed my first 'run' which was about five rounds of twenty seconds.

I thought I was going to pass out! I laid on the floor for at least twenty minutes afterwards, trying to get my breathing back to normal, what on earth was I thinking? There was no way I could do this.

I persevered, each run got a little easier, and my fitness improved. I even started to enjoy it. But I was doing too much – all the training on top of the usual stuff took its toll. I got a cold and then a virus, then another cold. This went on for nearly ten weeks. I could not train, could not do much at all most of the time. I felt like I was back to square one with my fitness, but this time it was different. I knew I could make a new start.

As well as the physical training for the run, I had started ticking other things off of my fortieth bucket list. Attending courses, reading self-improvement books. My support network was stronger and better than it had ever been in my life.

One of the courses I attended was 'Mindfulness for Stress'. I had started researching mindfulness in books and online, but the course really helped my understanding and showed me how to implement it into my life.

Mindfulness and meditation became a key part of my life and to living happier. The power of living in the now, being fully present in the moment, appreciating the world around me in all its wondrous glory has been life changing. This led to me rediscovering interests and passions, including yoga and photography which flow from the living in the moment.

My life looks very different from the start of last year. Recently I remembered one woman who said to me near the beginning of my journey that tiredness is a state of mind, that you can let it rule your thoughts or you can choose not to let the tiredness takeover.

At the time I thought she was talking a load of rubbish; how could that be? I got less than six hours sleep every night, and frequently less than four. Of course I was exhausted! For a long time, it became my mantra. Whenever anyone asked how I was, and sometimes even when they didn't ask, I would say 'I'm tired'. Well I still do not get any more sleep. Night times are still difficult. But it is different.

As a family we enjoy life. We go on adventures, we laugh together, and home is calmer and less stressful. I fit more into each day, each week than I ever thought possible. There is balance in my life, my cup is no longer empty, self-care features highly in my life, and we are all happier for it.

Mindset is a very powerful thing and we each have the power to control our own minds. My life is very much a work in progress and that is the way it should be, I have much to learn and I am enjoying the journey and the process.

Along the way I have met many inspiring people. Some have come and gone, some have become a significant part of my life. Life does not have to be perfect to be happier; you don't need to know all the answers. You do not need vast amounts of time. There is no need to solve all your challenges in order to find peace and calm, in the words of **Vivian Greene**

"Life isn't about waiting for the storm to pass...It's about learning to dance in the rain."

Chapter 7 - Denise W Saunders

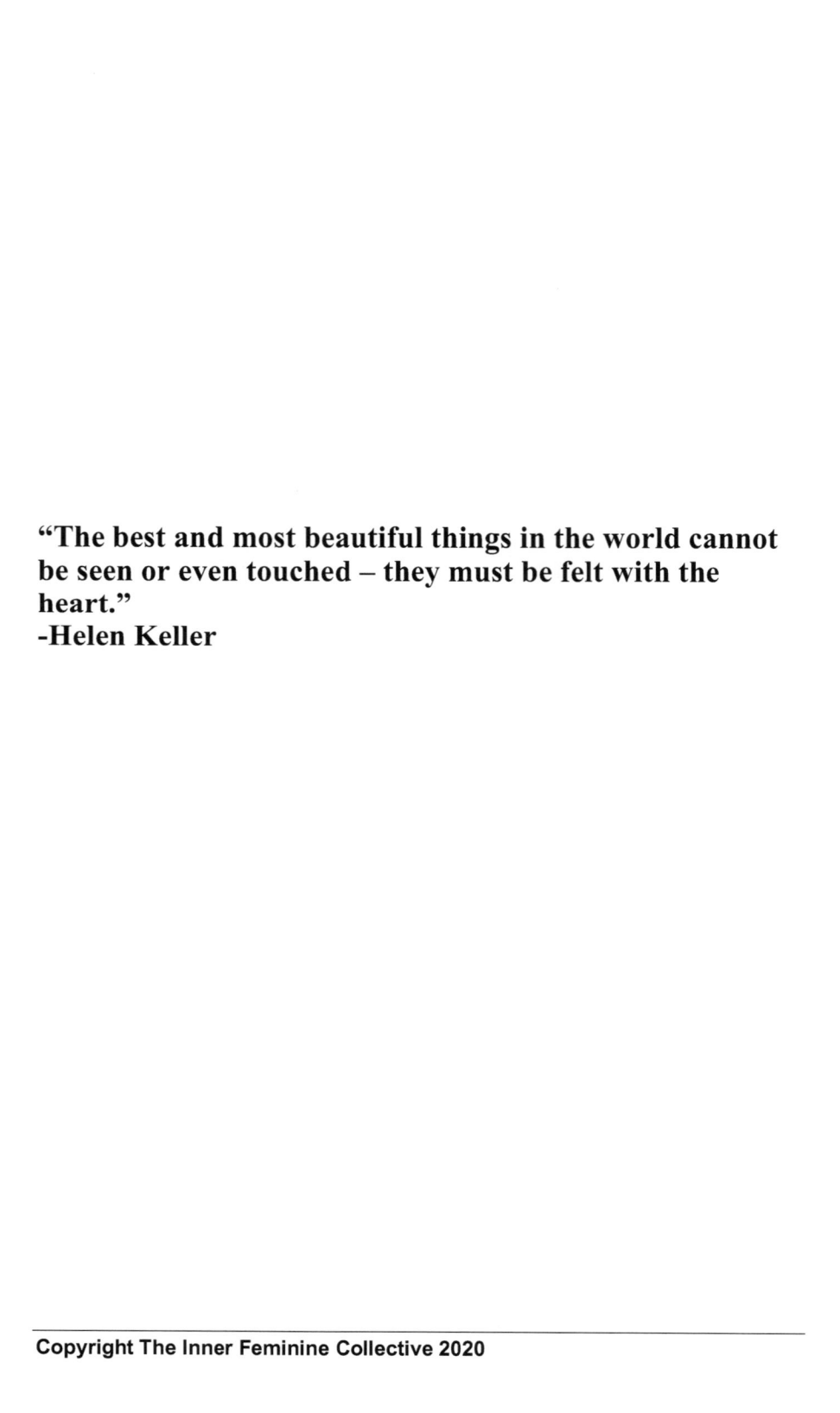

"The best and most beautiful things in the world cannot be seen or even touched – they must be felt with the heart."
-Helen Keller

I love learning about how our bodies and minds work. My favourite subject at school was Human Biology, and how we think, learn and develop as people has always fascinated me. I love a good medical or forensic drama, in books, TV and films. Those gory operations too!

It is not surprising that the professions I have chosen in my life have been health, education and therapy based.
For many years I was a Midwife working with women and their families.

Something that still amazes me is how we can have this funny little organ inside of us, no bigger than a pear, that has the ability to grow to the size of a watermelon worthy of its own scene in *Dirty Dancing* AND another human inside it!

The mighty *uterus*.

Then after nurturing and nourishing this growing human, this funny little organ will have developed the most powerful sets of muscles in the world that can contract and retract, getting thicker and shorter till our *new human* has no option but to head out of a place that common sense would say is *never* going to stretch *that* far! But it does!

Then it sort of all goes back to *normal* – well a *new* normal, I guess!

Moreover, we are capable of continuing to nurture this new-born into infancy, without any additional *equipment* other than our very own bodies.

We don't have to make it happen; it just is.

Yes, sometimes we need a helping hand, but women are super powerful just by being women. We don't have to prove this or justify what makes us women.

We are all unique, yet most of us share the same human form, with its funny, sometimes painful, unpredictable, ever changing rise and fall of hormones, seasons, and tides.

We are like an ocean, pulled by the moon, crashing to the shore or way out in the calm, still vastness. Sometimes a storm stirs up chaos, but we are ever the ocean with its deep, life giving water. We can be terrifying one minute and soothing in the next.

Sometimes our bodies do betray us. We have to endure painful, messy periods for a start. Sometimes our uterus is the enemy within. Our fertility or infertility can make us rage with utter anguish. **Why now? Why not?** Or it can fill us with the most abundant joy and ecstasy.

The pains of childbirth, should we take that route, are super-charging to our collective power because it involves the ultimate creativity, that of new life.

Because of the sheer size and scale of our power, women are revered by some and feared by others. Men and even other women may try to control us, but we cannot be tamed.

Not truly. Not completely. Not forever.

We can pretend all we like, to have complied, but who we are inside is always there. Like a caged bird, open that door for even a second and we will be out there, wings spread and flying high. We cannot be contained. In time we will all be who we are meant to be.

Women in all our divine, creative power.

I am forever grateful to have been with so many women at a crucial time in their own life stories. Most were joyous occasions, but occasionally times of great difficulty and sorrow.

I learned so much from these other women - the mothers - about the strength, resilience, wisdom, and power of womanhood. I learned from my teachers and mentors how to sustain and encourage this power during birth. I remember the awe I felt, and even in the darkest moments of loss and despair, this strength, resilience, wisdom, and power were evident.

Women survive and this too is part of the divine, creative power of womanhood.

When my turn came, I completely trusted in my own inner power, and knew that whatever the outcome, I would be safe and capable of being whatever I needed to be.

I felt super-powerful and believed in the divine, creative power of my own womanhood, and in the skill and judgement of the Midwives who were with me throughout. I would survive whatever happened. I would be okay.

In the not so distant past, the delivery room was the domain of women; only the mother-to-be, the Midwife or other experienced women would be given entry to such a sacred place.

But did you know that the word *Midwife* is not a gendered term?

The word *Midwife* derives from the Middle English *mid-wif*.

Where *wif* means wife or woman, MID means **together with**. Therefore, MIDWIFE literally means **with-woman**; that is, someone who is with a woman to assist her when giving birth.

According to one online dictionary, the word OBSTETRIC better describes a midwife's role, DERIVED FROM THE LATIN **to stand in front of** the mother as her baby was born. BUT… That is NOT how it is at all.

Midwives don't stand *in front of* women and their babies. They stand *alongside* them.

This is what I learned from becoming a Midwife. *Women* are the experts in their own journey into motherhood and beyond, but the Midwife is a knowing friend. Someone to be there with, for and *alongside* the mother, and ultimately her family and significant others, to reassure and encourage. To share the divine, creative power, passed on through time.

Midwives are with women from the first signs of pregnancy till 28 days after birth (and occasionally longer).

Midwives are the expert in the *normal*, which like life itself is not the same for everyone, but follows a similar pattern.

They can spot potential problems and know when to call on medical assistance to safeguard mother and baby.

Midwives can deal with emergency situations, including breach birth and multiples (twins +).

Midwives advocate for women by understanding her needs, wishes and worries, to speak up when women do not have the words to speak for themselves. Even if the Midwife is not themselves a woman, there will be empathy and rapport.

Copyright The Inner Feminine Collective 2020

The Midwife will be *with* woman.

This too is part of the divine, creative power of womanhood.

So, why am I telling you all this?

I believe that what is truly in someone's heart never leaves them and being a Midwife is part of who *I am*. When I had to finally give up my registration, I cried. I felt a true sense of bereavement. Even now after over a decade, I am in my heart, still a *Midwife*.

So how did my move away from my heart's true calling come to pass?

In a moment of what now seems like sheer madness, I was tempted away to become a Teacher in a Secondary School. I really believed I could use my skills and experience to help shape the next generation of carers and parents of the future. In hindsight I was not *reading the signs* clearly, and I never thought for a minute I would ever not go back to it.

I found myself in the strange world of the Secondary School. Despite being newly qualified with lots of passion and self-belief, over time I was battered into submission by a system that I did not believe in. I found myself scrutinised far beyond any scrutiny I had experienced as a Midwife. I found the unbending establishment stifling, and my creativity nose-dived.

Whilst my experience and expertise as a teacher grew, and I really loved some aspects of it, I began to feel out of step with my *true* self. Over time my confidence was eroded. I began to tell myself I was no good at being a schoolteacher, after all.

The truth was it felt inconsistent for me because it really wasn't *who I am* at my core.

The *old* me – the *true* me - was being erased by the *me* I had chosen to pretend to be, in order to fulfil what I thought was expected of me. Away from school, I was far more authentic, but even that was being influenced by how I felt at work.

But still I stayed.

So, why did I stay? What exactly *was* it that kept me there? I felt un-valued and unsupported much of the time, and I was so tired. It is hard work to pretend. Extremely unhappy and frustrated, I felt trapped. I could see no easy way out.
I now see the relationship I had with my job, as like being with an abusive, coercive partner.

I didn't want to be seen to *fail*. I didn't want to give up something I'd worked so hard for, and invested so much time and energy in. Therefore, I allowed myself to continue being beaten and downtrodden, so I didn't have to say, "*I give up*".
I still loved teaching, but the whole education system did not really fit me, nor did I fit it. I was trying to squeeze myself into the role like a round peg into a square hole.

It felt like I really should have had the bravery and courage to stand up to it, to change it, when in reality I should have had the guts and gumption to **WALK AWAY**!

A memory recently popped up on my Facebook profile from around that time:

"Could run away... Fortunately it's home time and I can go and rid myself of the toxicity some people have deposited on me. 6 days and counting."

I remember the circumstances around that comment. I remember the year I'd had. I remember how demoralized I felt. I remember experiencing some of the most challenging types of behaviours from my students, day in and day out. It was relentless.

I was just about clinging on, but was so close to the edge that now, looking back it is terrifying to think just how near to breaking point I really was.

I was massively at what we might call *effect*; in other words, affected so much by the outside influences of what I was experiencing, I was in a stressed state much of the time.

When we find ourselves completely overwhelmed, exhausted and without any clue as to how to get out of our current situation, we are no longer at *cause;* in other words, we become powerless. We are not in charge of ourselves and our power is given away to other people, other circumstances, and events, and it gets caught up in a big jumble of emotion.

This was happening for me because I couldn't see that I had the *choice* to stay or leave.

Emotion in this sort of situation is almost always an effect of outer stimuli, but it is not the reality for everyone involved in the events. It is *real*, as in, you *feel* the consequences. Oh yes, that bit is vividly real for the individual experiencing it. And it can feel like nobody else understands or even cares, because their reality is so different to your own at that time.

This was certainly the case, and I wasn't even sure who was a friend or a rival amongst my colleagues. It is so easy to find yourself slipping into paranoia, mistrust and ultimately feeling completely alone in the situation. And I did feel very alone at that point.

But as a mentor of mine has said many times, this is the *map* and not the *territory*.

When we are in this less resourceful state, our thoughts, feelings and ultimately our behaviour and actions, are being guided by a faulty roadmap… our internal GPS is dodgy! Old thoughts and feelings re-emerge too, from those other times when we felt powerless, overwhelmed, and impotent. We then go off in old directions. New, straighter, smoother roads are forgotten, and we can go the long and bumpy way round to what feels like nowhere. We become a *victim* of circumstance.

You may have heard the term *self-fulfilling prophesy*, which is when your expectations about another person eventually result in the other person acting in ways that confirm the expectations. Well that was me… my inner voice was screaming,

"Nobody knows how this feels. Nobody cares about me."

So of course, the behaviours I *perceived* in others, just confirmed to me that they didn't care, the students didn't respect me, I was a rubbish teacher because of it. And so on...

This was purely an internal dialogue, made up by my mind in response to the strain I felt.

In times like these, we are at danger of coming completely unstuck. When times like these persist, we are not in a fully resourceful state, and this can have a knock on effect on every area of our lives, our relationships with ourselves and other people, our productivity, our health and wellbeing, our happiness, joy and fulfilment.

Left unattended, this can lead to ongoing mental health problems such as depression.

Left unattended, we can become self-destructive and sabotage our ongoing happiness.

Left unattended, we can reinforce old beliefs we hold about ourselves, our ability, our worth. Decision making becomes even more difficult and the cycle continues.

Thankfully, I had the summer break to look forward to, and I knew that I would find healing and solace in my home, family and friends. I could look ahead to the new school year and the new timetable, which would surely be less arduous than the year that had led to this.

But something else had happened that summer. I had made a decision and taken *action*.

I started the process of walking away from this abusive *partner*. I started to formulate my *escape plan*.

I took back my divine, creative power.

I knew that I could not face another year like the one before. I knew that in order to protect my ongoing well-being, I needed to force a change in circumstances, for nobody else could, or would, do that for me. I would go back part time. The drop in pay was worth every penny.

I would have more time to start thinking about what I DID want to do. For *me*.

Everything I *chose* for myself beyond this point, was done in the state of *cause* and not *effect*. I was no longer a *victim* and I was back in *control* - and it felt so much better.

I attended a life-coaching workshop, which gave me some clarity about where I needed to be. I wasn't entirely sure of the route, but the direction was clear, and the destination was set in my internal GPS map.

I took a chance by starting up a network marketing business and the following year I reduced my working week further, to just 3 days a week… and then I did leave my teaching job! I was able to take a very small pension early, so I resigned and embarked on some new learning, and now, my perspective has taken a complete shift.

I was able to make life-defining decisions and ultimately take a new road with my up to date internal GPS sat-nav installed. I still sometimes feel unsure of the route ahead, but I am loving the journey! And I know my guide map is based on my own core values, my divine creative power, and not just a jumble of emotions as a result of how someone else's agenda affects me.

Life is enjoyable again and the future is exciting. I can be my true self once more, and I accept myself lovingly and wholeheartedly, perfect in all my imperfections. I believe in my inner creative power and that I can make a difference in the world, just by being me.

I manage my own diary, supply teaching and examining when I can, but without the added pressure of a contract. And I am enjoying being a Grandma to our gorgeous Grandson and taking on new opportunities as they arise, in all sorts of diverse ways. I was even *Mrs Claus* at a Christmas event last year and Storyteller for an online Kids Mental Health *carnival day* recently. All great fun and having an impact on the happiness and wellbeing of others.

Copyright The Inner Feminine Collective 2020

I discovered new skills and trained with *Your Life Live it®*, a global coaching and training company. So, by developing my business as a personal coach and mentor, I can now put my life and job experiences to good use, and my talents won't go to waste.

It is an honour to see the change people can make for themselves with a little help, and how they might achieve their own heart's desires, and live a life of purpose and happiness.

And, although I may not be a *Midwife* in the same way as before, I can certainly still be *alongside* other women in their divine creative power. I can still advocate for women who may not feel ready to stand in their own power, and when they *are* ready, applaud and cheer them as they *give birth* to their creation, whatever that may be.

I can still watch and learn from other women, too. There are some fantastic women leaders out there and I am inspired by and learning so much from them, all the time.

All of this fills me with joy and a sense of value, so I now feel more like a *round peg in a round hole*… such a better fit and so much more satisfying to the soul.

What creative magic have you yet to unleash on the world? Whatever it is, be your true self and just go for it. You *can* make a difference and live a life of purpose and happiness, just by being *you*!

Believe in YOU, make decisions, and take action… and claim your own divine creative power.

Chapter 8 - Kirsty Pearson

"You are braver than you believe, stronger than you seem, and smarter than you think. But the most important thing is, even if we're apart…I'll always be with you"
A.A. Milne

Until recently, I had spent most of my adult life feeling out of place, disconnected. As though I do not quite fit in anywhere.

I had good friends, a loving family, a job I liked and a social life that ticked all the boxes. But there was always something not quite right. I was not comfortable in my own skin. Not quite sure who I really was. As a result, I never felt secure. I felt like a fraud, an imposter. Waiting to be found out.
In my younger years, I drank more than I should to take the edge off my awkwardness and sought validation at every turn; not trusting in my ability to make decisions, always wanting other people's approval, wanting them to like me.

I realise now that I had become disconnected from my inner magic, inner light, and innate wisdom. The part of myself that connects me to a higher spiritual power, the universal energy that connects us all, that transcends life and death. When we love and connect with ourselves, we communicate with the world around us with an open heart. Open to the gifts the universe has to offer us, including the wisdom of those who came before us. We connect with others from a place of love, seeking to understand not only our experience of the world but theirs too. Seeing our differences as an opportunity to learn and grow rather than divide.

The road to me reconnecting with myself was messy, dark, and very painful. It began with the birth of my first son Thomas. Thomas was born with a life limiting condition, one that was never diagnosed. He was truly a one off, an angel child, as my Granny would say.

When Thomas was born, I became aware of an energy that I had long forgotten. I felt a connection to something much bigger than me for the first time in as long as I could remember, and it felt calming and supportive. It was as though I was being looked after and guided. At the time I could not have explained it or put it into words, but I was very aware that I was not alone.

On one occasion, we had moved from the neo-natal unit at Leeds Hospital to the Special Care Baby Unit in York and I remember one of the nurses going to find a mobile to put on Thomas's cot so he would have something to look at. That evening before I left, I wound it up and it began to play 'You are my Sunshine'. I was immediately comforted. This was my Great Grandad's song and I knew he was close. I remember smiling in acknowledgement.

Then, as we were preparing to bring Thomas home, I met a friend for coffee. She had bought Thomas a wind-up Giraffe toy, which also played 'You are my Sunshine'.

Another sign from my Great Grandad. Bringing comfort, and a feeling of peace. Knowledge that in amongst the fear and uncertainty, there was also deep love, connection, joy, and happiness. It was as though he was reminding me that I had a choice – to live in the fear and worry of what was to come and be consumed by emotion, or to live in the present. To spend my time loving and connecting with Thomas, creating precious memories together.

I recognised that while our future together was uncertain, no-one could really say what would happen and when. Thomas had already defied many expectations.

If I spent my time living in the fear and worry of what was to come, I would be missing out on the time we did have together, distracted by emotions instead of experiencing the joy and happiness of being together.

Missing out on the gift of life that we had been given. I chose to be present in each moment, to take every second that we had together and make it count – to feel and experience every part of our time together, the scary overwhelming parts and the joy, love, and connection. I felt guided and supported throughout, every part of this journey was meant to be.

The night that Thomas passed away, I remember carrying him to the little room at Martin House Children's Hospice. This is a special room where your child can stay after they have passed away. I became really concerned about where his spirit would go now that he had died. I worried whether he would be safe. Who would look after him now?

I remember feeling him in my arms that evening as I slept. As though he sensed my worry and stayed with me to support me through the initial transition.

I remember waking the next morning and intuitively knowing to open the windows and the door. To allow him to pass through and join our spiritual family. I spent a week in the little room with Thomas, tending to his body and preparing for his funeral.

Carefully selecting the clothes for his final journey. Choosing mementos to send with him to remind him of us and guide him safely to our family on the other side.

This time of transition was deeply healing, allowing me to care for his body, his earthly vessel. And to come to terms with the fact that his spirit, his soul, had already departed. The experience taught me that a lot of beauty and peace can be found in rituals. In love and connection, and a belief that we are a part of something much bigger than ourselves. We are one with the universe and we are all connected, whether we are earth side or on the spiritual plane. We are still together.

I felt this strongly in the first year after Thomas' death. I felt this energy around me all the time. I lovingly referred to it as my gaggle of geese, because I could feel this energy was made up of a group, engaged in deep, sometimes heated, discussion of how to support me.

It was a loving energy. It felt soothing, protective, as though I was being fussed over. As if they were taking turns to check in on me. Especially in the darkest of moments. When my grief was overwhelming. In the long hours of the night when my thoughts would keep me awake. I would see little orbs floating around the room and I would know that my spiritual army had my back. They were there with me, holding and supporting me.

In these moments, I did not have the energy or the focus to maintain the blocks and walls that I had built up around me throughout my life. The walls that had limited my connection to this universal energy. This was when I was able to feel it the most. I became aware of the beautiful energy that has always been a part of me, around me, and I allowed it to support and guide me when I needed it the most.

After the first year, my gaggle of geese quietened down. I sensed their presence less. I began to process my grief and found ways of managing it, moving through it. But before long, some of those old blocks and walls crept back, preventing me from feeling connected to that energy so deeply.

Missing that connection, I began to seek out spiritualists, and mediums, in an attempt to re-connect. To re-discover that sense of support. I was told that my geese were still there but that I needed them less now. They did not have to make their presence known as much, but that they were always there in the background. They still checked in from time to time.

Around this time, our second son Noah was born. I saw evidence of them checking in again. I saw orbs on the baby monitor, around me in the early hours of the morning when I was sleep deprived and struggling.

They were always there when I needed them, and I always felt them when I was at my most vulnerable.

A couple of weeks after Noah's birth, I came down with the flu. And I discovered that I had developed a deep-rooted fear that if everything was alright with Noah, then I would have to die. I was not consciously aware of this fear, but it led to me uncovering a lot of deep-seated beliefs I had about the world and about myself. Including that I did not deserve to be happy. That I was not worthy of a happy ending. That it was a choice between my child's life or my own. I could not have both.

I worried that I was going to die, and then about who would look after Noah if I did. Then I would feel guilty that Thomas would think I did not love him as much, because I did not want to die and be with him. The internal dialogue was intense and all consuming. I searched for my gaggle of geese, but I could not find them. I could not tap into that energy no matter how hard I tried. I felt alone and scared.

But that intense experience of anxiety would lead me to connect with myself in a way that I never had before in my adult life. Clearing away those blocks and walls for once and for all. I had no need of anything standing between me and that universal energy or my own wisdom and magic.

I began to challenge the beliefs that I had carried around for years. I suddenly saw that many of them did not even belong to me! They were not truly how I felt about myself but came from messages that I had picked up from other people along the way. I had collected them and made them my own. They were never about me. I could see that I was holding on to them, nurturing them as though they were *my* truth. When they really came from other people's experience of the world.

These mis held beliefs were affecting my ability to love and connect with the most important person. Myself. By challenging them and picking them apart, I began to connect on a deeper level. This led to me beginning to love the parts of myself that I had previously shunned and loathed. That I often chastised myself for.

I was able to transform my anxiety from a big scary monster, into a friend. To respect it for the internal alarm system it is meant to be. I was able to create space to nurture and love myself, to make my wellbeing a priority and in doing so I found the connection I was so desperately seeking.

This was not an easy transition and my path was filled with overwhelming internal dialogue, self-sabotage, and panic attacks when I really thought I was going to die! But with each step I took, I gained more knowledge and used it to continually check in with myself and challenge every self-limiting belief I had laid claim to over the years.

I faced the parts of myself that I had previously hidden from view and I showed them love. I connected with them, worked to understand them, and learned to turn fear into curiosity. Now when I feel my anxiety starting to build, I take the time to pause and reflect and ask:
"What is happening for me right now? What is the feeling or belief that is triggering this?'"

I opened up to memories of when I was growing up before I built the walls and assembled the blocks. I realised that when I was growing up, I had always been connected to that universal magic. Aware of the energy that surrounds us and flows through us.

My Gran and Aunty told me stories about the spiritualist church they attended and the messages they received. How they had seen or sensed things. How much more there was to our existence. How we are connected to a much bigger force than our own. Gran would tell me stories of angel children. Children who were sent to earth to deliver gifts and messages.

Aunty would speak openly about being guided by a higher spiritual energy and our connection to those who have gone before. My mum also shared her experiences of this. And I remembered, as a child, being aware of things that I could not quite explain, of signs and shifts.

I recalled feeling a strong sense of connection, of a higher spiritual power, something bigger than me. But the connection had been buried under layers of stuff that I had absorbed over time. Buried under beliefs that I was not enough, that I was too loud or too much, that I was not quite right. I had disconnected from myself and in doing so had disconnected from that higher spiritual power.

Thomas's death had turned my world upside down. It pulled everything I believed about the world, and my place within it, out by its roots and threw it down in front of me. I felt lost and vulnerable. Like a piece of me had died too.

A piece of me did die of course. That bit of me that existed in the false reality I had created, where I was not enough, not worthy. For a long time, I was torn between the person I had been and the person I became after Thomas.

Like a caterpillar retreating into a cocoon, I withdrew. From friends, and from everything I once believed about myself. I knew I could never go back to the person I had been before. Thomas' life and death had irrevocably changed me.

That caterpillar has everything inside it that it needs. The time spent in the cocoon allows it to transform into something stronger and more beautiful. And the butterfly soaks up energy from the sun and takes flight.

Over the last 8 years, I have sorted through all those old beliefs. Replanted the healthy ones. Buried the ones that longer serve me. I have planted a whole bunch of new and amazing beliefs and values. These are firmly rooted in love and connection. Blocks still appear, triggers still occur. That is normal, they always will. But from this place of love and connection I can sense which ones need nurture, and which ones should be dug up before they take root.

I examine them with an open heart, with genuine curiosity. My internal alarm system still operates, but it knows it is heard, seen, and understood. New blocks and triggers are less likely to take root, most are naturally weeded out through this process. Leaving room for growth of the beliefs and values that nurture my soul and bring a sense of peace and contentment, of alignment with my soul purpose.

I am stretching my wings, ready to fly.

Thomas brought me back home to myself, guided me back to the path I was always supposed to follow, but had strayed from. His love, life and passing set me on a journey which would lead me to reconnect to my inner magic. To the light at my core that connects me to my innate wisdom, and to that of all those who have gone before.

Through finding myself, I also re-established my daily connection to that higher spiritual power, the universal energy that I had been seeking. My heart is open all the time. Where I once saw vulnerability and weakness, I see love, strength, and connection.

While Thomas cannot walk by my side on earth, he is still very much a part of me and I a part of him. Even though we are apart, we are always together and always will be. That is incredibly special.

All our experiences guide and shape us. They steer us towards our soul purpose. Especially the ones that bring us to our knees. The ones that we think will never move forward from. The universe and your gaggle of geese have your back, they are holding space for you.

No matter how dark it gets, always believe in the magic of you. Nourish your soul with love and acceptance, allowing your magic to shine bright and true. This is the light that will guide you on your way in times of need. And in those moments when you feel you have lost your way, when you cannot see your light – take a deep breath, pause and just be.

Tune into you, into your inner space and allow yourself to be open to intuition and guidance. Listen to your heart and surrender to the faith that your soul knows the way and it will hook you up with all the magic and wisdom you could ever need.

In the darkest of hours, you meet the most beautiful of souls – your own.

Chapter 9 - Amy Whistance

Copyright The Inner Feminine Collective 2020

"Freedom lies in healing. To love, accept and embrace all of who you are and in allowing others to love you in all your authenticity."
Amy Whistance

Hi, my name is Amy. I am a mum of three, I am 35 and I live in a village just outside of Aberystwyth. I am a holistic therapist.

I am sure that many of you introduce yourselves in a similar manner.

In introducing myself to you I am also reintroducing myself to me. How many of us declare who we truly are when we say "Hello." Perhaps we are not entirely sure who we are. Or we are not comfortable enough to truly share. Or maybe we have repeated the same introduction so many times that it has become what we believe.

That thought is where it all began for me. Kind of.
I am not my name. I am not my age. I am not just a mum. I am not where I come from and I am not what I do for a living. But stating those things feels safe. No one can pass judgement and pick fault with the facts.

Observing other women, unafraid to be themselves, and openly expressing all that they were and what they were about, I would cringe. "Too much", my family would say. "Head in the clouds", "reckless", "embarrassing".

Unknowingly, I carried the fear of being "too much", "too deep", "too out there" with me all my life. When I created my business, I stripped the word holistic from it because I was worried it would seem too "hippie" and that no one would take me seriously. It felt like trying to advertise McDonalds without mentioning burgers!

Here is my real introduction:

Hello lovely. I am a healer. I have always been drawn to heal and it is my life's purpose. My life, with all its twists and turns has led me here to guide other women. To love themselves, to know their worth, to find confidence. To experience freedom, to acknowledge their strength. To lift them up. Empower them to thrive, not just survive. My motivation is seeing the light go on in others, the light that they have dimmed to fit in, to feel safe.

I am a walking contradiction. An introvert, but the life of the party. A deep thinker but easy going. Borderline obsessive and passionate but scatty and messy. Compassionate and nurturing, A warrior but sensitive. The list goes on.
The beauty of this is that I now realise we get to be all of it. All those moving parts. Every damn cog. There is no box.

In my early twenties I read a quote that had a profound impact on me.

"Tell the story of the mountain you climbed; your words could become a page in someone else's survival guide".

I thought 'maybe'. But I was not ready. Struggling mentally, I felt broken down, worn out and emotionally chaotic. I could not look in a mirror without crying. It was not that I hated my physical appearance, I was just so lonely. I felt I had no one to turn to and my only comfort was myself. I would look at my reflection and say, "I can't carry on like this, I don't know what to do". And something within would tell me "you can, and you will". Instinctively, I would encourage myself.

I was stuck in victim mode. Understandably so.

I was sexually abused from 4 to 14. Found myself mixed up with a grooming gang. At the age of 15, I lost a daughter due to Edwards syndrome. Then came an abusive marriage with a bigamist, and children.

I would love to say that I ended that marriage because I found the strength to. In truth it was simpler than that.

Someone else paid me attention and gave me the affection that I craved. This set the pattern. I lurched from one unhappy relationship to another, scared to be alone and never finding what I yearned for.

I could not see that what I needed was already within me. That I would not find it until I learned to value and respect myself enough to avoid relationships that I knew would end in pain. I ran from anyone who truly cared and respected me and chose those who appeared a challenge, that cheated, were aloof.

I started to feel my life was coming together. I started a university degree. An overnight decision after my father told me that I would be deemed practically illiterate without a professional qualification. He also told me that no ''respectable man" would ever accept me with my children, and that I would have to settle for the best I could get. Boy did I believe that.

My biological father was not in my life for the first 18 years. Yet his words held so much power over me. I took them in and lived as if they were true. Living my life like a series of car crashes, one after another. Treating myself with a total lack of respect.

I was so far from what I now know is my soul path. Years spent off track trying to prove a point because I allowed someone else's belief to become my own. Lost in misery, just one bad situation after another.

I was hounded by the ideas that had been drummed into me. That children of single parents are disadvantaged, poor, poorly educated, poorly disciplined. I was hell bent on ensuring that no one could say that of me and my children. I was ashamed to be in my position. I compensated by being harsh when disciplining my children. Not abusive, but very critical and obsessed by how others would judge me as a parent. Scared to fit the stereotype.

I spoiled my kids too. Wanting them to have everything. This became so important to me that I became an online sex worker during my last year of university. I felt empowered.

As though I was battling the demons from my past. I was promiscuous. It felt like rebellion. That I was taking control of my body and my sexuality. I felt emboldened by my new earning potential. I was finally going to prove "everyone" wrong. My children would have everything they wanted and would be happy. I had left my childhood trauma behind. I was in complete control.

I think we know that I was wrong! I giggled as I wrote this, oh the stories we tell ourselves!

I became detached from myself and others around me. My life became a tangled web of lies. Imagine lying to everyone about everything. Nightmare! You get the picture.
I am unworthy. I hate myself. This became the recurring theme of my life. I had no boundaries, I was ashamed. Living in a cycle of cognitive dissonance.

I have reached rock bottom many times, but somehow, I always found strength to pull me through. Deep inside I knew there was more, much more.

Since childhood I have always been drawn to religion. Or rather, the concept of faith. The power and strength that faith inspires in believers. Faith so strong that throughout history, millions of people have been prepared to die for it. I have tried a few religions on for size. Unsure of what I was searching for. A sense of belonging? Or my idea of the strength provided by faith?

As a family, if we were asked to choose a religion on a form, we would have ticked Christian. But we were not actively religious. So, in my teens I explored this further. I tried to view the bible as lessons taught through stories. But I struggled with the magic of it. I remember once getting in a debate with a Nigerian friend of mine. "You don't believe in miracles?" she exclaimed. At that time, I didn't.

Some years later I converted to Islam. The Quran contained the old and new testaments, so it was an easy and natural transition. I became very involved. Praying five times a day, fasting etc. I voluntarily wore hijab because I found such sanctuary in that anonymity. My practice in the religion brought me closer to faith because I was participating fully.

It felt like the right path, but so much did not sit right, did not align for me. I found the sense of faith I had been looking for, and that brought strength and power. But I felt disconnected from a lot of the content.

I went on to study Eastern religions and many of them resonated. I researched pagan based religions and felt at home. Eventually I realised that while religion fascinated me, I was more spiritual than religious. I felt something bigger than us existed. How could I look up into a night sky and deny that miracles exist?

One night, waking at 3am, I felt an urge to discover more about the science of the creation of our universe. Wanting desperately to believe that there was something more, but my doubt creating confliction. I researched thoroughly, but each time I found an explanation I would think "but what about before then"?

I remember speaking to an ex of mine, he was Catholic. I asked him if he really believed in God and he said "I hate the thought of being alone, that it is all on me. What a huge weight to carry". I understood that. I felt alone.

As a child I always felt that someone was with me, sometimes it would scare me. I would hide under my blanket at night. Most of the time the feeling of presence brought great comfort. I would talk and explain. People would ask who I was talking to. As I got older, I saw it as a coping mechanism. The time came when I could not sense it anymore. I felt a huge sense of loss. But from time to time it reappeared and brought great joy.

Some years ago, a friend of mine discovered The Secret. She made sudden drastic changes in her life that I respected but did not understand. I watched the film, but it did not make sense to me. I wasn't ready. But gradually I saw some truth in aspects of it, and I began to adopt some essence of the law of attraction into my life.

Then I read a book by Paul Mckenna called "Change your life in seven days". It didn't! But it did suggest to me that it is possible to rewire yourself. I tried numerous times but nothing stuck. I was the queen of procrastination, never completing anything. I didn't recognise it at the time, but fear was stopping me.

Then I had what I would call a significant emotional breakdown. My anxiety, depression, and unhappiness with the life I was living spilled out. People around me noticed and I felt a total loss of control. I could not keep up the façade anymore.

This was possibly the best thing to ever happen to me. I signed up for counselling. Something I have returned to many times. But I was never really honest with them. Still holding back for fear of judgement. It was unsettling and I would go back and forth. Something else I did not complete. I would open up Pandoras box, get to the part where they would explain how I was wired, conditioned. But I could not stick around to understand how I could change.

I had the tools but no support network to help me use them. One of the counsellors gave me a book called "They fuck you up" and it explained the connection between your experiences as a child and how that manifests in adulthood. How the limiting beliefs and conditioning of your parents create the basis of your own. I was devastated.

I had spent so many years trying to run from the stereotype, to prove that I was not my past. The book showed exactly the opposite.

I decided to go it alone. I knew I needed to heal. For me. For my children. I realised that my behaviour would mould my children. As they grew, I saw that in them, and it broke me. I realised that I was worth the change too. Something inspired me to go back to the law of attraction. I started making huge changes in my life.

I reconnected with my inner guide, source. I learned to take inspired action, to take giant leaps of faith knowing that I would be held. I walked away from my big money earning career overnight. Something I had tried to do many times before but failed. I went from a high paying career to £0 income, but I was held.

I journaled who I wanted to share my life with, how he would make me feel. I joined an online dating service and I found him straight away. He is the love of my life and he unlocked so much for me. He listened to my story and loved me all the more for it. He has a respect for me that I never experienced before. He loves me unconditionally and never lets a slip of doubt cross my mind. He spurs me on, no matter how mad my ideas!

We have faced difficulties. Soon after we met, his father fell seriously ill and he passed away six months later. It had an incredible impact on my partner and his mental health. But it bought us closer together. I was still healing too, but he continued to hold me. For the first time in my life I was able to accept love.

We visited his dad in Wales for six months and each time I returned it felt as though I was coming home. It is where his father moved to after his mother died. It is where my family is originally from.

I felt drawn to the area and after a string of events, and some manifestation we found the perfect home, the ideal workplace. It all came together, and we moved our family to Wales.

My healing still needed some work. This showed up in my career. I still felt inferior and unworthy. Anxious when meeting new people. I knew there was more to do but wasn't sure what. I joined a manifestation academy. One of the modules we had to work through was self-love. I didn't think it was something I still needed to work on.

I thought, "no amount of affirmations is going to make me feel any differently about x, y or z". My subconscious did not believe these things. But self-love is something I preach about in my business. It is a core value. I was talking the talk, but not walking the walk.

I started to note how I spoke to myself. I heard my Size 4 teenage daughter refer to herself as fat. I saw her measuring her wrists, talking about getting a boob job. I told her she was insane, that she was beautiful. I saw her trying to please people, including her boyfriend. "I don't understand" I said to my partner. "She had a completely different life to me, why does it feel like the repeat button has been pressed?"

Then it hit me like a ton of bricks. How in the world could she value herself, how could she recognise her own worth, see her beauty, appreciate her qualities when all she has ever seen is me putting myself down, berating myself, holding back in fear, despising myself. How could I tell her to practice self-love when I still could not do so?

I needed to do this for myself. I started my journey. Again. I began to rewrite the stories that I had always told myself and to live by example. To thrive and not just survive. To speak my truth, my whole truth. To be all of who I am because we get to be. I needed to find my magic and after searching far and wide I found it within me.

At last I found the path to healing and happiness. I learned to love myself, value myself. From that came everything, a powerful connection to source, a complete and absolute faith. Belief in inner guidance and trust that I will always be ok. There is bubble of love and joy that surrounds me and lifts me. I discovered my purpose and an ease and flow of inspiration that helps me on my path.

This is the heart of it all. The first steppingstone. Learning to love yourself, believing that you are worthy. Knowing that how you think, feel and what you say matters. Being strong enough to have boundaries and keep them solid. Being able to let the right people in, allowing yourself to be loved, feeling worthy of love that is kind and gentle.

You do not need to be liked and loved by everyone.

You do not have to people please to be accepted.

You do not have to say yes to everything and everyone.

You must feel able to stand up for yourself.

You are not responsible for how others think and feel.

You can be you and be loved, respected and appreciated.

Your tribe will find you.

There is no space in your life for anxiety, lies, or emptiness.

You do not need to look for anything outside of yourself.

It is all within you.

You are capable and you can do this.

Self-love is the start of your journey, being you, all of you, your authentic you.

Are you ready to reintroduce yourself to you?

Who are you?

What journey have you been on?
What lights you up?
What are you passionate about?
What are you drawn too?

Hello lovely, I am honoured to meet you.

x

Chapter 10 – Michelle Maslin-Taylor

"There are no difficult decisions in life. Our soul always knows the answer, the only difficulty comes when we don't like the decision our soul has already made, or our logical mind wants to analyse it"
Michelle Maslin-Taylor

There are no difficult decisions. Yes, you read that right - there are NO difficult decisions. There are consequences, people who may get hurt, people who may be disappointed, expectations you fail to meet but there are no difficult decisions.

Once we accept that we could all make our lives so much easier, free from the torment and anxiety of mulling over and over the same points trying to make a decision that our soul has already made for us.

You see, we all have this amazing sense of true north, our soul guiding our way. Inner wisdom, intuition, our higher self, god…. However you want to name it, we all have it but so many of us have lost touch. I believe it is the root of mental health ailments such as anxiety and depression. That unshakable feeling of discomfort in your life, unease, and discontentment.

What is missing?

Why am I not happy?

It is time to claim back your inner guidance and find your way to happy.

Settle in, its story time. I want to share with you my own journey and how what goes around comes around when it comes to decision making.

As a child I was innate intuitive, as most children are. Through my teenage years I was drawn to all things "woo", "new age", or "spiritual" - crystals, essential oils, tarot cards and books on meditation and clairvoyance.

I still have a book I bought at a charity shop, my Chinese health balls from the new age shop in a nearby town and an oil burner with a yin yang symbol on. My room was filled with wall hangings draped over furniture of Hindu gods, Sanskrit symbols, and the symbol of Om. I vividly remember sitting cross legged on the floor, staring into a mirror with a candle in front of lit, following a ritual in my book, looking to connect to guidance.

I recognise all these things in my life now as a yoga teacher, now understanding the symbolism of the Ganesh wall hanging that I chose, the obsession with the yin yang symbol and the symbol of Om. I meditate daily, though not with a candle in front of a mirror. These things are ingrained in my everyday life and I now see how my intuition guided me to them all, but back then, they were just weird.

Over time, I hid this side of myself away, ashamed to be "different", bullied for being shy and weird, wanting to just blend into the background. Cue intuition showing up again.

When it came to the end of secondary school, I needed to choose a university and degree. It was easy; yes because all decisions are! I fell in love with the University of Essex when I visited, a leafy green outdoor space, not too far from my home, so I could get back often, and I knew exactly what I wanted to study - A joint honours degree in Creative Writing and Psychology. All set.

However, the career councillor and my family questioned what on earth I was going to do with that degree. What job will that lead to? What is your career path?

I had no idea. I just knew that was what I wanted to study, not why or where it would lead me.

My final year of sixth form was, from what I can remember, a blur of being bullied at school, underage drinking at the weekends, missing a lot of classes due to the bullying and feeling completely disconnected to what I was studying.

I was a shell.

I was deeply in to disordered exacting already, in my need to control and try to fit in. I was depressed. I felt hopeless and useless.

I believe now that this deep depression stemmed from not allowing myself to follow my path, instead being caught up in all the "should" of what I should do and who I should be.

Unsurprisingly given how much school I missed; I did not get the grades needed to make it to that university place. I knew it was the one and was not interested in going through clearing to find something else.

So I buckled up, applied to college and got ready to do a year's intensive to retake my A-levels, this time taking psychology and sociology to add to the English Literature that I passed with flying colours. I could feel deep inside that this course was worth it.

A year later and I nailed it. I had the grades; I had my place. BUT in that year, I let myself be talked out of the course. I still did not know what job I wanted to do with it.

Did I really want all that student debt just to study something I enjoyed without a purpose? Could I really manage living away from home? I was so shy, and nervous - I would never cope.

Once again, ignoring my gut and letting fear and expectations take the lead I sheepishly resigned myself to "taking a year out" to choose a more career focussed degree and got a job. I am sure you can guess, but that year did not lead me to finding the degree for a career, it led to me to a job where I stayed. I forged a career as a web developer, training on the job and then spending 20 years working as a developer.

Have you had an experience like this? Where life just kind of happens around you and all of a sudden, it's a decade (or two) later and you wonder where it's gone and what you've done?

Decades of feeling like something was not quite right.

Decades of ignoring the niggles and nudges from the universe.

I still felt the calls from my soul, managing to sprinkle in nods to it through my career as a developer - focusing on promoting accessibility and inclusive design, to focus on people and, in particular, on those for whom the internet was a lifeline. I found ways to utilize my call to write through user research, reporting and writing up reports summarising information for our teams.

But the niggles continued, and they got louder, with my soul practically shaking me to listen and the universe providing shoves to move on to something else.

For women, I believe there are often turning points that lead us back to our inner guidance. It might be a milestone birthday - 30, or 40, 50, 60. It may be motherhood, or the decision that you do not want to be a mother. It might be an unexpected redundancy or illness.

Often these are the catalyst to reconnecting with ourselves, to our purpose and desires. Our inner wisdom.

I turned 30 while pregnant. I had exactly what I wanted - baby on the way and "secure" job but something felt out of place. My first pregnancy was relatively easy; baby arrived safe and well, despite health issues and a breech birth, meaning an early delivery. However, I struggled with motherhood. I found it hard to bond after a c-section, as it was the complete opposite to what I had in THE PLAN.

I found it so hard, feeling as though I had completely lost my identity, without the job that had kept me from hearing the niggles for so long. But I did what I did best, I set about following rigid routines and life planning to get a sense of control back.

In hindsight I can see that I was yearning to make a change, to live a relaxed and flowing life and that falling back to my controlling and planning was leaving me unhappy.

I got back to work but it was not cutting it, leaving me unfulfilled and bloody miserable to be honest. I wanted to be home with my baby and wanted something else… still no idea what but knowing something was missing.

Why is it that we can spend years, decades even, living with this feeling? Society seems to have trained us to just walk the line, make a plan and stick to it - no matter what the cost.

At what point do we begin to believe that our life needs to be planned out decades in advance?

For me, sticking to a plan stopped me from being "distracted" by the random ideas and niggles that my soul was sending me. Do you have those? They pop into your head and keep popping up at the most annoying of times.

The life plan that I had in my head, was to stay on course with my chosen career and that I would have my second child shortly after the first. I wanted two under two, close in age and best of friends.

That did not pan out.

There are often things we cannot control in life and this was one of them. Life was leading me on a different path and forcing me to relinquish control.

My fertility journey is a complete story, all on its own. Suffice it to say that between various tests, depressing results, a missed miscarriage and a 30% chance of IVF success, a beautiful baby girl arrived, naturally, four and a half years after the first.

This was my turning point.

Things changed when this miracle baby came into my life. I changed. I wanted more from my life, I knew that I wanted to make a difference in other people's lives and to show my girls that it is possible to live a life that feels good, to love your body, to be yourself, to let go of what doesn't feel good - all through leading by example.

A renewed yoga practice, and then pregnancy yoga helped me so much through these years and one day, speaking with my pregnancy yoga teacher, now a good friend, I realised that she had left a corporate job to retrain as a yoga teacher. She did not have this lifetime of fitness behind her, she had been like me - in an office job until she decided to change.

Immediately I felt this joy inside me! I was meant to retrain as a yoga teacher. I knew it in my soul, it kept popping into my head and seemed crazy, but I could not ignore it and started by simply googling yoga training courses.

With all big decisions comes fear, and I certainly felt it. But I felt so strongly that this was my path, it was a calling. An unexpected miracle pregnancy shortly after my daughter meant that my plans went on hold, but I felt so connected to the journey ahead of me. During my third maternity leave I was made redundant when the company went in to liquidation. The universe was clearing the path, freeing my time and energy. Divine timing.

Fast forward to today: I am running my own business.

I am a yoga teacher, a reiki practitioner, and an intuitive coach. I create online courses that integrate yoga, meditation, journaling, personal development, crystals, and essential oils. The many years I spent as a web developer have given me the skills to be able to create my content online with ease and joy. Yes, joy!

Joy in the creativity, joy in the seeing my vision come to life, joy in seeing it change women's lives as they also create joy in their own lives.

I write. I write about all the things I love - yoga, mindset, health, and emotions included. I have been published in a major spiritual magazine this year, just in time for my 40th birthday, and I cannot believe my eyes when I see my name on those pages.

I am constantly learning. I read about, learn about, and write about psychology every day. I love learning and sharing.

Remember that joint honours in Creative Writing and Psychology? Those crystals and oils and meditations in front of the mirror? That is basically my daily life now and the tools I use daily to help women in my business. Every Single Day.

They are all intrinsically linked to the core of who I am and what I am here to do.

It is funny how we always know the way.

This is why there are no difficult decisions, because the answers are always already inside of us; we are being divinely guided, IF we listen.

All those years ago, I knew what I wanted to study because it lit me up, it made me happy and fascinated me. But logic and other people's opinions and all the whys? and wheres? steered me off course. I let the logic, the reasoning and the worry get in the way. I ignored the niggles until they manifested into redundancies (several), and health issues and begged me to listen.

I was always looking for connection to guidance, not realising it was already there.

But I found my way back, and you can too. My house now, looks much like my teenage bedroom did - filled with crystals and oils!

If you do one thing for yourself, stop ignoring those gut instincts.

Start to notice when something feels exciting.

Start to read more about what interests you.

Start to spend more time doing things that you love, or that excite you.

You may not know where it is leading but your soul does.

The greatest tool in manifesting the life we desire is feeling. Feeling joy and excitement and a purpose. That all comes from following the nudges without questioning where they are leading you.

Enjoy the ride!

Chapter 11 – Gemma Alexander

"She decided it was time to let go and move forward. So she packed only the best of what she had been through: the fragrance of burnt hopes, that fine nectar distilled from her fears and the precious collection of each sweet bruise etched on her soul. And off she went arm in arm with the universe.
– Neelam Tewar.

Once upon a time a beautiful baby girl was born, with a head of golden hair, blue eyes, and a heart full of love and light. Straight out of a fairy tale, her parents, the King and Queen of the eighties, were mesmerised by her, by the pure potential in her soul. What would their golden girl grow up to be? A doctor or a lawyer. Their little girl would change the world!

They were sure of it.

She worked hard at school - because that mattered. Knuckling down, trying her best. She had to work hard if she was going to achieve the very best in life, and doing her best made other people happy.

What happened to that little girl?

Eventually she became disillusioned. Her golden hair darkened; the sparkle faded from her eyes. She worked so hard, all the time, trying to keep up an ideal, a dream, to make everyone happy and achieve success. She became a teenager who was tired of working hard all the time. She had become distracted with making other people happy while she was miserable and lonely.

When I was ten years old, I genuinely believed the world was my oyster. I believed I could achieve anything I set my mind to. I believed in fairy tales; in fate; that everything happens for a reason. In the Spring of my life, everything was shiny and new, dripping with the dew of possibility, illuminated by the spring sunshine. The colours were so bright. All I had to do was to dream, to believe, and I really could change the world.

Now as I approach forty (shock horror!) I wholeheartedly believe all these things again. But with an added dimension, an Autumn perspective, the same picture, but with a golden hue. But for that time in between, those twenty-five years, a quarter of a century, the Summer of my life, I got stuck. I was lost in the chaos of life itself. It was not that I stopped believing in magic; or that I stopped experiencing the awesomeness of nature, the beauty of sunrises and sunsets. It was more that my focus was elsewhere, my energy drained. With hindsight, I spent the Summer of my life stuck on that rollercoaster. So many ups and even more downs, so many stories and experiences that shaped and changed the path I was on. Sometimes for the better, sometimes not.

I became a mum for the first time at the age of twenty-one. I raised my son to look for the magic all around us. Although I was young and single, I did not want anything to hold him back. My beautiful boy, who pulled me out of the first major dip of my life's rollercoaster. I was determined that he would grow up believing that he could be anything he wanted to be. When my second child, my daughter, was born almost a decade after her big brother, my eyes were opened for the first time about how much I had missed in my son's life. All the school invites I could never attend due to work. I realised there was more to life than rush hour traffic, wrap around childcare and constant fatigue. My children mattered more.

After my maternity leave ended, I opened my own bookkeeping business. But instead of achieving balance, I was constantly exhausted from working all hours, from juggling everything, and the cracks started to show.

Looking back, I see the lessons I needed to learn from each of these experiences. They have guided me to where and who I am now. But then, it felt like I was stuck in a never-ending downpour interspersed with lightning flashes and thunderbolts. Inevitably the daily grind of life, the slog and toil of work, marriage, children, housework, and debt. It all beats you down. Pulling you lower and lower, and when there is no-one to catch you when you fall, you just keep falling.

There are many inspirational quotes about getting lost and being found again. For twenty years I have ridden that rollercoaster; played lost and found. All while filling my phone camera roll with quotes about finding myself, transforming myself, and moving on. Heartache, heartbreak, relocations, new friendships, old friendships, new relationships, single motherhood, illness, starting my own business, marriage, divorce. All the ups and downs of life that most people go through.

I have not had any harder a time than anyone else. I hope many can relate to my struggles and find comfort in not being alone in them. Because we all experience moments of absolute bleakness. Feeling consumed by darkness and scared of not being able to find a way out.

Yet most of us do!

Looking back, I can see the cycle repeating over and over. I had to make the choice to get off the rollercoaster.

Copyright The Inner Feminine Collective 2020

Now I look up and look ahead instead of always looking back. Now I choose peace above all else. Because when you have suffered in the darkness, there is nothing more important than staying in the light once you find it again. It is enlightening. And empowering. To get to this point was hard. And it took really hitting rock bottom to force the change I needed.

Having my youngest was the big turning point in my life. My pregnancy was physically hard. Looking after a toddler, as well as a new baby, added to the physical toll and my marriage hit a real low point. Without any emotional support from my husband I muddled through alone. I was very lonely. I had no close friendships. There were no colleagues checking in on me during my maternity leave, which I had had with my daughter. I was already exhausted, already on a downward spiral.

Then, during my pregnancy, my Grandad was diagnosed with terminal cancer. Instead of blooming, and cherishing the anticipated arrival of my little boy, I was camped out on the floor by Grandads bedside. Reliving memories and making the most of what little time was left. Physically and mentally, I was running on empty.

Amazingly, Harrys' birth was an incredible experience. All 10lb 7oz of him, delivered at home in my living room.

With only gas and air and an incredible midwife. It was primal; it was powerful; it stirred the wild woman within me. Mother nature in all her glory. It was raw, painful, and beautiful. All wrapped in a bundle of new baby softness.

I had been called reckless for choosing a home birth, accused of endangering the life of my unborn baby by not going to the hospital. I was told it was a selfish dream to choose a home birth. Most people will never experience the deep roar, the primal force of nature, the connection with mother earth herself. But I have. She gave me strength when I could not push any more. I was tired and exhausted, but she supported me and encouraged me to dig deep and bring my baby home. Mother nature bared her soul to me, connected with me in a way not many people experience with the marvels of modern medicine.

In that moment I was blessed and guided, and more connected to my higher self than at any other point in my life. I was stronger and had more courage than ever before. It was life changing. A spiritual awakening. And it would change the course of my life, in time.

I took my new one-day-old baby to meet his Great-Grandad, his namesake. Everyone joked that he was like the hulk, born the size of most three-month olds. No-one could believe I had given birth to him at home and survived to tell the tale.

Yet here he was, the amazing little man that I had brought into this world, a pure soul, full of more love than I have ever seen in a child.

My grandad died 6 days after Harry was born. He clung on to meet his seventh great grandchild and we shared some special moments in those final days.

Most new mums suffer the baby blues. It is a normal part of motherhood. When the hormones rush through your veins, the deluge of milk floods your breasts and you can't pee without it hurting! Baby blues on a downward spiral with the loss of a loved one was catastrophic for me.

We were all consumed with grief. There was no-one rallying to see the new baby. No friends rushing to visit. My husband was in his own dark place, a million miles away from mine. I was alone and went from the highest of highs to the lowest of lows in a matter of weeks.

There was no one to hold the baby so that I could steal a moment's peace. There was no one to rock him so I could catchup on some sleep or take a much-needed shower. I was so overwhelmed with life that I began to shut down. I retreated into my own world. Wearing a smile, I pretended that everything was normal.

But as soon as I was home again, I gave in and the darkness consumed me. I felt trapped. I could not breathe. I could not rest. There was no peace. No escape. I had to solider on as a mother must. I was determined that this mama bear would not let her cubs down. I gave them my everything. All my love and every last bit of energy I could cobble together. I lost contact with friends, excused myself from family gatherings and social situations. I nearly lost my business. I crashed and burned, and my light went out.

Where was that wild woman when I needed her? She had appeared before when needed. Why had she not re-awoken, enraged with her powerful lust for life. To re-fuel and re-energise me? What good was she if she would not come to me in my hour of need and rescue me? If I could not seek refuge with her when I needed her strength.

I was stuck in a rut, just doing enough to make it through each day until bedtime. When I would lie awake and question my life, fuelling my anxiety and depression. I was so unhappy, in so much pain. There was no-one to talk to or to turn to.

Feeling raw and emotional took its toll and my marriage failed. Even at the darkest of times, there is always light if you choose to seek it and I found it in my children. I consumed all of that joyful new baby-ness. I watched my toddler learn to become a new big sister and relished the changes I saw in her. Tucked away in my retreat I felt safe with my babies. Nothing could harm us.

It was too hard to reconcile that my highest high and my lowest low had occurred within these four walls, the four walls where I now felt trapped. I left my husband and moved out of our family home with the children in tow. I exclaimed we were starting a new adventure. I thought I was making the best decision to protect myself and my sanity.

Looking back, it was a hibernation, I was a mama bear who felt the winter approaching and retreated to my cave, my safe, neutral space, with my cubs. A place of love and protection. In my solitude I was able to start on the shadow work I had needed for thirty years. An opportunity to re-invent myself; start over again, as the person I truly was deep down inside.

Moving out started me on a quest to find my inner light and bring it to the surface again. To wake that warrior wild woman and grow into her skin, to become the woman I was always destined to be.

That was when I discovered mindfulness. It flickered, a candle in the darkness, showing me a way back. It felt like Spring was finally coming and this mama bear did not have to hide out anymore. Everything that had been overwhelming before, brought little hints of joy now.

I fell in love with doing the dishes, consumed by the moment, the scent of the soap, the warm water, and the feel of the silky bubbles on my skin. Watching the birds out of the kitchen window, appreciating the clouds and the blue sky again. Doing the dishes became a daily high, something to look forward to.

Mindfulness infiltrated my daily life and brought colour back to where everything had faded. Mindfulness led to me practising gratitude and day by day things got better, life got rosier. I took comfort in the robins or the butterflies in the garden, a sign of a loved one visiting.

With my newfound positive outlook, I accepted an invitation to my high school reunion. Everything I had been through, up to this point, had shaped me into the awesome woman, business owner, single mum, home educator, I had become. I was empowered. I could take this confidence and walk through those school doors with my head held high ready to shout about all I had overcome to get here.

Only I didn't. I walked through those school gates and was transported back into my 14-year-old-self. Scared, anxious, nervous, my confidence disappeared. The teenage me that always worked hard, harder than everyone else seemed to, that was never good enough.

Until I walked back through those school doors, I had no idea that I have felt lacking and not good enough throughout my entire adult life. Perhaps it was the all-girls grammar school education where grades and academic performance were held in higher esteem than wellbeing.

Where we were pushed, not guided, to achieve top grades, to maintain the schools league table performance. Pushed to continue on to university and join further alumni so the school could claim that achievement too.

By the school's standards I was not a success. I do not have a degree. I am not a partner in a highly successful accounting firm. I do not juggle a career with a happy marriage and have children who are on the school football team or spelling champions. I do not have the dream house in the dream postcode with the dream car.

Back in the hotel after the reunion, I had to deal with those seeds that had been planted in my teenage mind that had become twisted and rotten. Success is not dictated by which school we attended. Not measured by how much money we have, or which postcode we live in.

Mindfulness and gratitude had brought me out of the darkest time of my life. But I had not realised the power of my limiting beliefs, how they had been holding me hostage for half my life. I realised that only when I conquered them, would I be able to unleash my wild woman, and step into my full power.

She had not left me, but she was trapped inside my mind. All those niggles and nags had built tall walls around her. It was time to start knocking down those barriers to my own success, to my own peace of mind. I began meditation, affirmations, hypnosis, anything, and everything I could consume to break down those walls and let my inner goddess breathe again.

I began a coaching program which introduced me to the power of the moon. And that was a real lightning moment. Not just a spark, a whole lightning storm. Letting go of years of baggage, forgiving those who had hurt me and situations that had harmed me for my peace of mind, not theirs. I began to feel the power and truly trust in the magic and the universe again. I started chasing down all the dreams I had for years. Like owning a caravan! I began diving into opportunities presented to me, like being a part of this amazing book project.

Autumn is my favourite time of year. So, it is appropriate that this is my favourite time of my life so far. Now I have the confidence to choose where I want to spend my energy. My foundations are solid, my offspring have sprung, and I am choosing to enjoy the golden colours of my autumn. To harvest the ripe, ample fruits of my labour that I have worked so hard and tirelessly to cultivate all my life so far.

I have my own bookkeeping practice that I run from home, around my family life. To the old me, success looked how my school prescribed. But it looks totally different to the new me! I am successful. My business is approaching its sixth birthday - not many small businesses survive this long. I am proud that like me, it is constantly evolving. Not only surviving but thriving.

I realised that I find joy in the simple things. That spending time and energy focused on those things raises my vibration. My children, our animals, music, nature. Helping people in my business. Spending time with like-minded women. That is where happiness lies.

I have discovered the importance of being part of a tribe. Of how those further on in their spiritual journey lift you. We rise together. Being a part of this project, The Inner Feminine Collective, broke down those final barriers and my wild woman has stepped out into the light. There she is on the cover of this book.

Where my wild woman took centre stage for the first time and for always!

Chapter 12 – Jules Sutton

'Stop overthinking, quieten your mind and you will hear the nudges you need to hear; your innate wisdom always has your back!'
-Jules Sutton

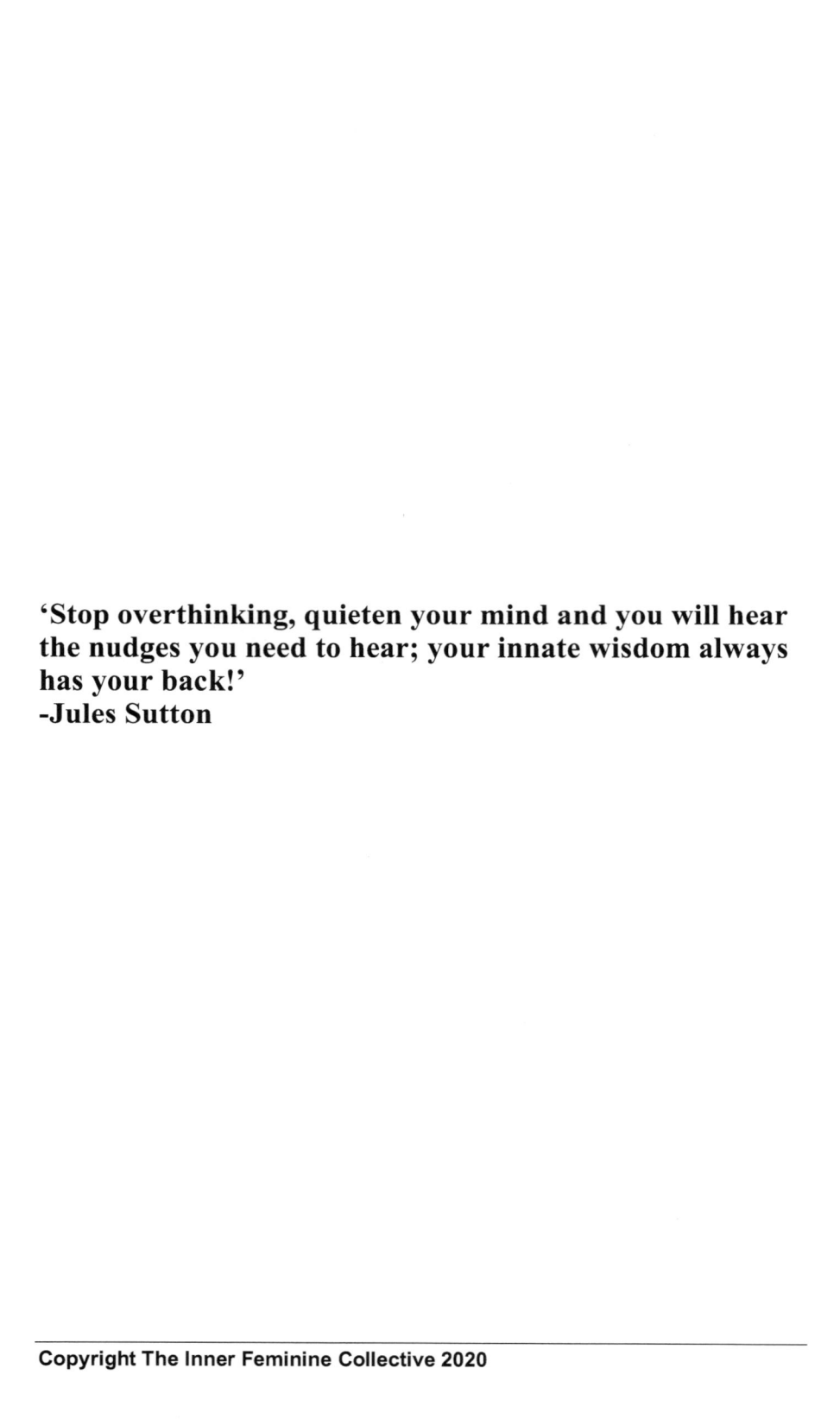

Gut feeling, intuition, inner wisdom….do you have it? Do you notice it? Ignore it? Challenge it? Does it scare you? How many times have you either regretted not listening to that nagging feeling, or been eternally thankful that you trusted it?

During my lifetime I have always been aware of what I thought was my gut feeling or intuition, but very often I have ignored it or over-ridden it by overthinking! I'd get the 'pang' and the 'feeling' to either do something, or not do something...and then I would over analyse and think through the potential outcome of doing or not doing what the 'pang' suggested I do or don't do...then the moment was very much lost!

What saddens me, is realising so much later in life that this innate guidance system, this inner wisdom had my back all along…but I hadn't trusted it. Instead I had spent all my time trying use my 'intellect' to make decisions. This invariably meant that I talked myself out of everything, as there is always a reason to be found not to do something.
So, what woke me up to the fact that we all have this innate system working for us, all the time?

Two pivotal moments where the guidance system was so loud and clear that something in me knew 100% to shut up and do what it said. Without question.

The funny thing is both these pivotal decisions were monumental ones for me. So huge, that one would expect involved a huge amount of thought, and weighing up of pros and cons. Maybe even a SWOT Analysis! But no. These two decisions were the clearest and easiest decisions I've ever made. This coming from someone who can spend hours upon hours researching holidays or online purchases without ever actually committing to a decision or a purchase!

So, what were these decisions, and why were they key to me finally understanding that something inside me has my back and can be trusted?

Decision 1. The Marriage Break-Up.

Panicked into a marriage, aged 27, because I had no confidence in myself and my friends were all getting married. Pretty dumb eh? Being brutally honest; I knew I had made a mistake on my honeymoon. That feeling inside me, 'the pang' told me I had royally fucked up. Shit. But who wants to put their hands up to that after a magnificent wedding and admit that they had made a terrible mistake? Not me!

So, I quietened the noise inside and carried on with blind optimism and denial.
'It'll be fine!' I told myself manically, daily. 'I'm sure all marriages have these issues.' 'I know, let's have a baby, that'll help!'

I think it was obvious that my family and friends were aware that things were not all rosy in the garden. But my denial continued with a chirpy 'no of course I'm fine, it's all good, yes of course we're happy!'

I was suffering from depression. I knew I had made a terrible mistake but admitting it, even just to myself, felt worse than the lie I was living. I was well and truly stuck. In a prison of my own making.

To the outside world I looked like I had it all.

When my daughter was two years old, I took a new contract job. There was a great bunch of women, all a similar age to me, in the team.

One day, I was sitting by the lake near work with one of my colleagues. We were eating our packed lunch and watching the swans on the lake. She suddenly blurted out that she was so envious of my life as she was single and would love a nice family home, a husband, and a child, like me. She saw a picture of my life and thought it looked perfect.

That was the first time I said out loud that it was all a lie. This was the kick up the arse I needed. Seeing another woman looking on enviously at my (fake) life and wishing she had it; that was it! I blurted straight out that I was unhappy and hated my life and my marriage.

To say she was shocked was an understatement.

She literally looked at me, and looked again, and I could see that she could not quite compute the 'story' she'd told herself of the life I had, that appeared to represent everything she felt she was lacking.

It was quite a moment for both of us. We sat and looked at each other afresh. She shook her head, I shrugged sheepishly and explained that this was the first time I had said out loud to anyone that I hated my life; but mainly I hated the fact that I was shushing my intuition and living a lie. A lie that other people like her were not just buying into, but envying!

I felt a strange sense of relief. It was fascinating. Watching her expression change as she looked at me; slowly processing what I had said and having to mentally re-adjust her picture of me and my life. The life that she had just told me she envied.

I felt a sense of relief at letting out the truth at last. But within minutes I started to feel a little panicky. What have I done? What have I said? I could feel 'the pang' inside me revving up and wanting to be heard. 'Finally, she has admitted it! Finally! At last we can start sorting this mess out!'

'Oh god' I thought. 'I've said it. I've awakened that mad 'pang' inside! Now what?'

I put these thoughts to bed for another 12 months. The final straw came on a "dream" family holiday to Florida with my Dad, Step mum, half siblings, my husband, and our 3-year-old daughter. Spending 10 days in each other's company was painful. Beyond painful. I realised I could not continue. I wanted to be with anyone but him.

We were so different. Everything that made me 'me' seemed irritate him. We were polar opposites. He was an unbelievable pessimist and I was a bubbly optimist (when I wasn't feeling depression and despair!) He was an early bird; I was a night owl. He liked a plan, and wo betide anyone who deviated from said plan. I liked spontaneity and adventure. He liked to allow 5 hrs for a 1 hr journey…I liked to allow 63 minutes.

On return from the holiday the 'pang' was back…but this time it wasn't just a pang. It was an ever-growing surge inside me that was screaming to be heard. One afternoon I was driving home from work and grabbed my phone, without thinking, and called one of my very close friends. 'Can you meet me tomorrow morning at Starbucks? I think I'm going to leave him.'

Ohmygod where did that come from?

Copyright The Inner Feminine Collective 2020

I didn't even realise I was going to call her, or what I was going to say until the words came tumbling out of my mouth. It was as if something else inside me took over!
A cocktail of emotions bubbled up inside me....

Instead of talking my way back out of it again, as I usually did, or disputing the 'you don't love him' feelings. Despite my mind cranking up the usual craziness: 'But what will you do? Where will you live? You are working part-time, how will you afford to buy a house? You will be alone forever no one will want a 33-year-old divorcee with a 3-year-old!!!' and so on, this time I felt a strange sense of calm descending upon me.

It was bizarre. I do not know why it happened on that particular day. I knew that I had made a mistake, but I had lived with it for almost 8 years. I had successfully ignored and overridden the pangs for all that time. I had always managed to 'talk' myself out of leaving (that conversation took place in my head by the way!)

Something was different this time and I cannot quite put it into words. I just knew. It felt like the Universe whispering directly into my soul. 'It's now. Do it. Just do it and trust that all will be fine.'

So I did.

And it was.

It was more than fine.

4 months after moving out I met my best friend, who is now my husband of 12 years, and we have another daughter together.

My life could not be more different from before and now if anyone envies my life and marriage, it is justifiable! This time it is all real!!

Reflecting on that experience, looking back, and feeling grateful that I didn't waste another year of my life living a lie is one of the most important lessons I have ever had. I lived in fear of all the 'what if's' holding me back from living the life I really did deserve. I vowed from that point on that I would trust my innate wisdom to guide me. It was also a great lesson for my work colleague and a reminder to me that other people's lives are rarely what we think they are, and this was before I was even on Facebook!

Decision 2 – Leaving my proper job!

The second time my innate wisdom made itself loud and clear was over work. I had worked in HR for over 20 years. The last 9 years, in a large Government Department. I was passionate about my work and loved the fact that I was known for being the least typical 'HR person' most of the managers and directors had ever worked with. (This is a good thing).

However, over the years the continual changes in the political environment meant that the organisation was continually being pulled in different directions.

We were subjected to almost constant, seemingly pointless, restructuring, so were continually on an ever-moving change curve which became quite draining.

I was lucky enough to be approached to play a key role in a controversial pilot way of working and I was seconded into my dream job. I was so happy and fulfilled by the purpose of my work. But after 20 months, yet another change in Ministers took place and the plug was pulled on us. Another restructure when I was told my old job had been removed. I was given another role, that I had never wanted to do, at a location 1 hour 15 minutes' drive away from home.

I HATED IT.

I hated the journey.

I hated the office environment.

But most of all, I hated the actual work.

The work that normally filled me with passion; management development, coaching, facilitating workshops, training and so on. All this was taken away and I spent most of my time on the laptop looking at spreadsheets, and providing data to senior managers, that appeared to go nowhere and serve no purpose.

Anyone who is familiar with Myers Briggs (MBTI) or similar personality tests will understand that I was now working in a job that was directly opposite to my 'type'. The effect of working in a role that provides none of what you like doing, being or having, and requires you to work completely against your type is a guaranteed recipe for misery!

And miserable I was.

I have pretty much always enjoyed work and have never been one to suffer post-holiday blues or anything similar.

However, after 4 months of working like this I found myself driving back to work after a 10-day holiday in Croatia with tears pouring down my face.

'Shit, this isn't me! I don't do this, pull yourself together' I berated myself on arrival at work. I re-applied my make up to disguise the tearstains, had another word with myself and went into the building.

I sat down, opened my laptop, and looked at my emails. 345 of them. None of which I could give a shit about. I slammed the laptop closed and walked to the toilet.

I had another word with myself. The Monday morning Management meeting was starting in 3 minutes.

I walked into the boardroom, putting on my best smile. I was good friends with the Director, which was the only thing that had kept me going so far. He called me in to his office after the meeting. He asked how my holiday was and asked if I was ok?

He said he could see through my smile. 'No, no I'm fine its okay, all good, you know just readjusting after holiday I said, trying harder to make my smile reach my eyes.

He still looked unconvinced.

I paused. I felt a strong sense of déjà vu. And not in a good way.

Oh! I was doing that thing again. That thing where I chirpily try to convince people I am fine when I am very much not. Oh dear. 'Anyway, I told myself, it's just the first day back after holidays, come on be grateful you've got a job, think of the money and the pension!'

I felt slightly better.

He told me he had some news and poured me a coffee.
He told me he was retiring. In 4 weeks.

I kept myself together and wished him the best as I walked out his office.

I grabbed my bag and headed out to my car.

I drove to the petrol station round the corner.

Switched off the engine and burst into tears.

The one thing that made it even a tiny bit bearable was going.

I sobbed.

Then that feeling came again. The one where the message of what I need to do goes directly to and from my soul.

I will leave.

I am going to leave.

'But you haven't got another job…what about…etc'

I AM GOING TO LEAVE.

SILENCE.

Calm.

I drive back to the office and get through the rest of the day with a strange sense of calm.

I walk into the kitchen and tell my husband 'I'm going to resign. Tomorrow'.

His eyes widen.

He knows I've been unhappy, but I don't think he realised quite how unhappy.

'Umm, do you think you could wait until you find something else?' he asked tentatively.

'NO! I am afraid I can't. I cannot wait another minute'.

These words tumbled out of my mouth as if coming from somewhere else.

A little frightened voice inside tried to pipe up with the usual 'but what about the mortgage, you've been there nearly 10 years, what about the pension?!' But it was getting quieter and quieter.

I just felt the wonderfully familiar feeling of total calm in the face of a massive decision.

Luckily, my husband just looked at me and smiled. 'I can see you've made up your mind! I think we can manage for a bit; what will you do next?'

'I will finally work for myself.' I said.

Again, wondering where that came from.
'I'm going to coach women and young girls to help them fulfil their true potential and not live a half-arsed life like I did until I woke up and listened to my own innate wisdom.

Now is the time!

Copyright The Inner Feminine Collective 2020

And I did!

One of the messages that I share with my own daughters, and the clients I work with, is to understand and trust their own inner powers to guide them. You will never have all the answers, and if you wait to have them, you will never grow. I had no idea what would become of me when I left my first husband, or when I quit my job. But my innate wisdom made itself known to me and now I know to 100% trust it.

These are the two biggest decisions I have made and in both cases I acted purely on that feeling. Without really having a clue of what I was going to do next. I knew I was being urged to do it and I trusted that on both occasions, it was what I had to do for my own highest good. I only wish I had listened earlier. Maybe I just was not ready and still had lessons to learn.

My advice then; listen in, tune in but most of all TRUST.

Nothing comes from staying still and small. And living a lie because you are too scared to move into the unknown is not living. You are meant to be, do, and have a great time in your life – and your innate wisdom is always there willing to guide you, when you let it.

You will be so grateful when you do.

Chapter 13 – Kim Boyd

Copyright The Inner Feminine Collective 2020

"At the end of the day, we can endure much more than we think we can"
Frida Kahlo

I was born in Gateshead in 1958.

A sensitive child, I remember an incident in my infant's school when we were all sitting in a big circle. It was sharing, or story time, I think. And I noticed that one of the little girls in my class had no knickers on. I was so sad for her that I cried my eyes out.

I have remained this empathetic all my life. I hate to see people suffering. When Fusilier LEE RIGBY was murdered in London in 2013, it nearly broke my heart. I could not bear to think of his parents, and his wife and what they were going through.

I was the eldest of five children. My parents were kind. I always looked to my Dad to sort things out for me. Trusted him to take care of me and handle any problems that I ran across. I have always feared people in authority but back then, I knew I could always go to my dad for support.

When I was sixteen, I got my first job. I worked in a lightbulb factory, testing and packing lightbulbs. I remember on one occasion packing one faulty bulb in a pack. My supervisor went berserk, and I went home crying. I just was not strong, not able to deal well with criticism and authority. But Dad always had my back.

I realise now that I transferred this dependency to my first husband when I got married. But that support came at quite a cost.

I married when I was twenty-one and we had two kids. The marriage was not an easy one, and I know now that I was simply existing, not living. When my youngest was three I became quite depressed and my mum told me I needed a job.

I found a job as a domestic in a local hospital and the routine and just being out of the house helped me immensely. My confidence grew and then I found a job with a mental health support company, working with dementia patients, and I am still there after 26 years.

It is fulfilling work and I have embraced the job, growing with it, learning, and taking every opportunity that it presents. One of things I am most proud of is the opportunity to be present when one of our patients passes on. It is an honour to just be there, holding their hand and being present for them at that time.

Eventually my first marriage ended, but 17 years ago I met my second husband. He is the most caring, loving man I have ever met. He makes me giggle and supports me in everything I do. We are a team, and I can depend on him the way that I used to depend on my dad.

Three years ago, I was invited to a hotel in Darlington to hear about a range of skincare products and a business opportunity. The founder of the company, Susie Ma, was a finalist on Alan Sugar's The Apprentice back in 2011.

Although she did not win, Lord Sugar did invest in her idea and her company is now very successful. I fell in love with the products and was very inspired by Susie's story, so I signed up for the business opportunity, which is in direct marketing. I could run my own business while maintaining the job that I loved.

Being part of the company has helped me become more confident, and I love using and sharing the products. I feel better about how I look and feel, and I began to explore self-development as well.

Feeling braver and wanting to help my business grow I decided to attend a local Mums in Business networking group. It was a little out of my comfort zone, but I met a lady there called Mandy Nicolson. She was such an inspirational speaker! I started to want more, felt a need to expand my life. I was ready to grow, with the support of my husband and my new network of business connections.

I made more connections and began to explore my spiritual side. Something I felt I had neglected. My circle of support grew, and I felt more and more alive.

Then 2 years ago things began to shift at work. The Organisation brought in changes which led to huge changes in the management team. My initial reaction was that this was a good thing. A new brush sweeps clean. Change can bring good things.

The changes happened at the speed of light. More forms to fill in. New computer systems, which I am rubbish at! Online training instead of the usual in-house training. The list went on and on. And all this happened within two weeks. My mind struggled to cope.

There was constant disruption, with senior staff leaving the floor regularly for meetings with the clinical lead which left me on my own to cope with the residents. This included personal care and preparation of meals along with a hundred other tasks. My fear of authority and lack of confidence in my ability resurfaced.

Then something happened that shook me up and set in motion a chain of events that would truly challenge me.

Copyright The Inner Feminine Collective 2020

Two new students came to work on the unit. I made them welcome as I always did. It was a very busy time, and I was running on empty. The clinical lead was taking staff off the unit to have her chats, which left me working alone with the untrained students.

About a week later I went into work on a late shift and the clinical lead asked to see me. I was informed that there had been an official allegation about my treatment of a resident. She told me that the management were mortified as in my 25 years of working for the company, there had never been any issues. I was told to stay at work, but not to talk to any of the other staff about it. That there would be a formal hearing to decide what will happen.

"Stay at work and have this hanging over my head I don't bloody think so!" I told her. I told her that I would cover my shift the following day but then I was taking a week's holiday so that I could be with my husband. I am not sure who was more surprised – me or her!

The week I was off work was hell for me. Lots of crying and long walks to get out of the house. I was exhausted. It must have been awful for my husband. Then one night while we were sitting chatting about the allegation for what must have been the hundredth time, a light bulb went off in my head. In that moment something happened.

Something exploded inside me and I found my voice. I did not feel as though I had ever used my voice, or even had a voice. But I decided that this time I was going to speak up.

I wrote down every situation I had been put in and left to deal with myself. It felt fantastic to get it all down on paper.

There was a fire burning in my belly. When my weeks holiday ended, I went back for my first shift and I asked to speak to the clinical lead. She was pleased to see me back at work but was not expecting me to speak up.

"I have thought long and hard about this situation and it should be me putting in a complaint against you!!" I said. "I went through hell that week because of you and I take great umbrage at how I have been treated".

It felt so good to stand up for myself.

On the day of the meeting I was so calm. I dressed smartly, did my hair and my makeup went on perfectly. I took my own union rep with me and I went in with my head held high.

I cannot share details of the meeting of course, for obvious reasons. But let me tell you this. I was confident and answered every question with great passion. I knew I was OK. I believed in myself. It felt so good. I had never stood up and fought my corner against anyone in authority. I felt like a phoenix rising from the ashes.

It took a further three months, yes THREE months before I received a letter to advise me that no further action would be taken.

What have I learned from all this? When you are pushed into a corner your fighting spirit comes alive.

I have discovered that I can find peace, even with my monkey mind in full flow!

Now I write about how I feel.

I have been exploring my spirituality, learning to trust my intuition. Stepping out confidently and bravely. I ask for help when I need it.

I am feeling so much stronger and more confident.

Do not be afraid to speak up. Ask for help if you need it.

I feel so alive!

Chapter 14 – Jayne Holland

''You don't have to solve your whole life overnight. And you don't have to feel ashamed for being where you are. All you have to focus on is one small thing you can do today to get closer to where you want to be. Slowly and lightly, one step at a time. You can get there''
Daniell Koepke

During my time coaching people affected by a loved one's substance misuse I had the great pleasure to meet and work with Nada.

Nada, as beautiful inside as she is to the eye, possesses grace, joy and a serenity that bely the heartache and trauma she has endured in her life. It was Nada's birthday; the sun was shining, and we decided to hold our one to one session next to the waterfall in the Buddha Garden. We had date and walnut cake and coffee to celebrate.

The previous week Nada had had great reservations about approaching 65, fearing that she would be as close to 70 as she was to 60. The plus though? At least she was edging closer to retiring from the stresses and pressures of Corporate. "God willing", she had added when I suggested this.

During this meeting we talked about our visions for the future. Nada's was to return to her homeland to help the children devastatingly orphaned by war. I discussed my plans for a series of self-help books. We discussed our shared passion for equality and freedom of personal choice for our sisters in other parts of the world. And those that may be living in the UK and Europe too, but still with family repressing their personal choices.

I told Nada about my long-term plan to pen a trilogy that would, through fiction, once again highlight the continued plight of these woman and girls. I shared my dream that it may also make it onto the small or, better still, the big screen and spread the message even further. "If only dreams could come true Jayne" Nada sighed. "Oh, but they can" I replied. "It's all in the conversion". And then I set about explaining -

Dreaming is part of life, a series of thoughts, images and sensations occurring in your mind. It is a cherished aspiration, ambition or ideal, it is contemplating the possibility of doing something and for you to envisage and visualize. But a dream held captive in your mind will always just be a dream. So, don't leave it to fade and disappear. If you want it to become reality you will have to move it on. To those deciding upon a new direction **dream big … why not!** Your dream is your vision, the vision is your motivation. Conversion will be your success.

To the repressed across the world…help is coming…**continue dreaming and never stop.**
To the orphaned children… Nada is with you… **a dream has come true but keep dreaming little ones, for this is just the start.**

That afternoon Nada gave me permission to use her story in my first self-help book.

NADA'S STORY

I hope that my chronicle of Nada's journey will help others to rise if in crisis or at one of life's many crossroads and, soar higher than they ever imagined. While this story is specific to Nada's particular situation, if a reader is not travelling the same path, they will almost certainly know someone that is.

It is Nada's hope that her story may be helpful to those that find themselves in the helpless wilderness of living with a loved one's substance misuse.

She hopes that it may steer them clear of the mistakes that she made. Huge errors in judgement that she still questions to this day. She also hopes that it will make the reader question their loved one's actions and their own, guiding them to be more reactive in challenging this forced and unscheduled deviation from the direction of the planned journey together.

Hope that they will see going along with this deviation will be to circle round and round the issue and appear accepting of the situation. Hope that they will not base their focus on solving this monumental problem with 'hope'. Hope is essentially to wish for the outcome that you want.

In Nada's case hope was for the drinking to stop or at least to moderate, so life could return to normal for Kareem. To get Kareem back on track and limit the damage to his life. If Nada could stem this destructive flow, it was her belief that they could continue their journey and live out their dreams together.

If Kareem could take this huge step then, Nada believed they could put the past behind and move forward.
But this was Nada's hope. Whereas hope for Kareem was in the bottle and, devastatingly as with addiction, Kareem would resort to anything to drink from that bottle until it was empty.

And then to repeat and repeat until the body's defences took charge and, for that moment could drink no more.

At this point Nada and her children seized the opportunity to try to get Kareem back on the straight and narrow. Nadia was not qualified, but she assumed the role of counsellor, rewarding and encouraging Kareem's abstinence, however briefly it lasted.

However, she now realises that the draw of the bottle was much stronger than any love and support they could give him. And whether this abstinence was for a few days or a couple of weeks, as a family they found themselves back on the rollercoaster, realising that it had only really paused for urgent and necessary repairs.

It was after the rollercoaster eventually crashed that Nada had time to research. Involving herself in a structured learning process, attending many courses. She studied alongside other carers; the term given to those living with a loved one's substance misuse. Substance misuse, again the professional reference to alcoholics and those taking drugs. Sounds a bit harsh but, I suppose it says it as it is. It is after all a no-frills situation.

Two other words that Nada learnt along this learning curve …

Very simple and with direct and uncomplicated meaning. In fact, a lesson in two words…

To 'ENABLE' AND 'ENABLING'

- Enable - to give someone the means to do something
- Enabling - empowering a person to take certain actions

Nothing difficult to understand is there? But, in Nada's attempts to limit damage and embarrassment for Kareem and the children, she was in fact enabling Kareem to continue on his course of self-destruction.

She can see it clearly now though. By sorting out the chaos as it happened, Kareem never felt or suffered any consequences resulting from his actions.

So, where did it ALL start…

Nada admits to ignoring the early signs. It is odd how the heart can sway mind over matter, normalising questionable actions and behaviour.   So much worked in their relationship. There were great positives which, she eventually thought would wipe out the negatives. The heart won every time…it is called love.

If you live life as an eternal optimist with your glass not just half full, but overflowing, it is easy to persuade yourself that life is shining, smiley happy and a great place to be. During the work driven days of the 80's and early 90's optimism and glass overflowing worked. Nada was in the spring of her young adult life.

With a burning ambition to travel the world she had chosen a career to enable this. Quickly rising through the ranks, she enjoyed her role looking after first-class passengers for a Middle Eastern Airline. It was here she met frequent traveller Kareem. Nada's twenties were spent in the fast lane taking her on a global journey. Life seemed complete. Not only did she have the world at her feet, she had found Kareem, her soulmate, sharing the same interests and vision for the future.

Her thirties and forties brought great joy for Nada as she grew with her cherished Saleem and their daughter, Nura. She had taken a part time ground job with the airline, combining motherhood and career.

Relationship wise life was mix of straight and curve balls. There were the happy times and, like most couples, the not so great times but, on reflection the balance leaned more towards the happy.

However, from her mid-forties the cracks were really starting to show. Like a vase, knock after knock. No matter how carefully it is restored it will never be the same. Every knock weakens the structure, until it cannot be repaired and eventually it crumbles.

The big crumble started in the years approaching Nada's milestone 50th birthday. Princess Diana famously coined the phrase 'there were three of us in the marriage …'

In Nada and Kareem's case two had become three a while back. But it was not easy to determine exactly when.

Backtracking to the 80's and early 90's, the era of the Filofax and Yuppie, meeting places were wine bars and hotel lounges. Business lunches were a regular occurrence. When the office closed, it was normal to stop off in trendy bars to exchange business of the day.

As the Yuppie Club graduated to the Parent Club most toned down this lifestyle. Nada certainly did, although she still enjoyed her wine time. But Kareem did not make the transition.

The draw to remain in the past was even stronger. Alcohol was a permanent feature in and around Kareem's life; still stopping off after work daily, hanging out in the trendy bars of the City, often gravitating to night clubs and casinos. Saturday afternoon pub crawls, also leading back to clubs and casinos.

Sometimes Kareem would not make it home. When he did, a hair of the dog pre-Sunday lunch session would follow. Alcohol was always present at home and on holidays too. Drinking became a round-the-clock activity. Beer o'clock, wine o'clock became whisky, vodka, gin, brandy o'clock 24/7 …the devil in a bottle had won. It was now the dominant force in Kareem's life.

So, where do the partners and families go wrong?

At first, those closest to the drinker do not actually realise they are living with an alcoholic. Not until the addiction is well established. By that stage they are alcohol dependent, but in denial, thinking they can stop whenever they want.

Nada now realises Kareem had been a functioning alcoholic for many years. But Kareem's serious decline lasted around seven years. During this time Kareem exasperated every doctor assigned to him. Every one of them eventually admitting defeat and referring Kareem on.

When Nada advised the final doctor allocated that Kareem had switched to a practice closer to his new home, the young doctor's reaction was one of pure relief. The poor man immediately looked 10 years younger.

The family and close friends never gave up trying to help. There were counsellors, private and NHS, who could do nothing with Kareem and specialist agencies too.

By the time it becomes apparent that there is a huge problem it is often too late. The partner will suspect long before other family members do, and they will work behind the scenes to support and try to fix things.

There will have been one to one's and group meetings with doctors and special agencies, some with the patient and others without. And they will continue along this route praying that abstinence will prevail.

As the alcohol takes over, the alcoholic can become very difficult and dangerous to be around, in terms of causing injury to themselves and those around them, sometimes accidentally sometimes not. The collateral damage that ensues is irreversible. The aftermath can last a lifetime for partners, children, and extended family.

But, if we love someone, we can be blind to their actions. Anyone who lives with a substance user, whether the fix is alcohol, drugs, or both, will know that the pull of the fix is so strong that it overtakes everything else in their lives. They will go to whatever lengths that they have to; they will be manipulative and deceiving. Then there are the emotional weapons that they will unleash if they fear that their fix is threatened.

Essentially, turning a blind eye, or convincing yourself that things will resolve with the passage of time is to dig yourself deeper in. You have become compliant with the problem. So, on the occasions when we voice a … *hang on a minute moment* then, a decoy will deploy to intercept the threat of the challenge.

The substance user morphs into the 'black butterfly'.

Through time we recognise that a shift in power is about to occur and, that to continue the exchange would prove futile. Which is why we more than often resist the challenge so, once again we are 'enabling'.

Attack is their best form of defence. Sometimes this may be an act of humiliation to break or silence you. Substance users excel in the mastery of illusion by transferring their guilt to you. How they do it varies. They may be aggressive or emotional. Or they may frequently switch between the two.

One minute the aggressor, the next an emotional wreck. Yet when calmer and more lucid they are truly sorry and want to make amends. Playing on the emotions of those closest to them, their sad and despairing moments absolutely crippling those who love them. Many of Kareem's still haunt Nada to this day.

So, the day of reckoning…

May 2012 was when the big crash came. Their main income stream had disappeared overnight with the inevitable voluntary liquidation of Kareem's business, shattering the lives of a family who had been gradually destroyed in the years leading up to this.

A trio of estate agents visited, a For Sale board was erected, the cars were collected. Saleem, soon to sit his AS's, and Nura her GCSE's knew that by September they would be uprooted, and they would have to leave their friends and familiar surroundings behind them.

To add to the problem the once healthy finances were now replaced by credit card and gambling debt on a scale so huge that they would wipe out most of the proceeds from the sale of the family home.

There were restaurant bills unpaid too. Rent arrears for a flat Kareem had been renting for his mistress. A demand for a full terms school fee arrears arrived home with two mortified children and many other surprises landing on the doormat on an almost weekly basis.

In the aftermath of any hurricane comes the tidy up. But, where to start?

The first year was certainly a year of firsts. With the addiction spiralling and, the potential cost of Kareem's alcohol fuelled madness, Kareem's accountant and solicitor advised Nada to file for divorce to protect what little was left in the pot.

There were the liquidators and creditors to assist, threatening visits from a few aggrieved restaurateurs and one of the casino's henchmen! There were the worrying finances to manage until the house sold. There were the concerns for Kareem too.

Not forgetting the devastation suffered by Saleem and Nura as their watched their world unravel.

Kareem's drinking continued, now on an unprecedented scale. Their already broken finances were about to crash further. The Estate Agents had called with the news that the agreed sale on the house had fallen through. Desperately needed funds, now not available. Simultaneously, a letter arrived from a London Solicitors, instructed by their client to call in a £250,000 personal guarantee that Kareem had signed the previous year to one of his suppliers.

Followed a week or so later by two Casino personal guarantees, taking these paper promises to just short of £500,000.

Taking into account Kareem's condition at the time of signing, combined with the fact that the companies involved were fully aware how of how fragile he was, Nada was able to fight these actions through the courts.

The challenges of this first year spilled over into the second year and then, into the first half of the third. But by early 2015 at least the house had sold, and most of Nada's inherited debt paid off, she relocated to Northumberland with Saleem, Nura, two dogs, three cats, a rabbit, and an aquarium full of exotic fish.

By mid-2017 Nada had finally come out of the other side and was realising her dream working with the orphaned children of her homeland.

I spoke with Nada just the other day and told her about The Inner Feminine Collective and she was thrilled to bits that The Nada Story will feature in such a special book.

I have promised Nada that I will write my self-help books and again feature Nada's story, and, that I will definitely pen the trilogy to highlight the plight of our repressed sisters around the world. Nada has asked for the first signed copy and has said that she will look forward to watching on the big screen…no pressure there then Nada!

I have also given my word that I will remember to make time to walk barefoot in the sand and through the forest, to smell the roses, listen to the bird song and enjoy the beauty that surrounds me. Yoga and Pilates have been added on my list too. This delighted my spiritual and very dear friend. Nada you truly are a *Mother Teresa*. Thank you so much for granting me the huge honour of narrating your story.

Thank you also for your teachings of the simple joys of life. Fondest love always J xxx

To the lady out there yet to come out the other side...

You certainly will. Keep focused, have faith, set your boundaries and, believe in yourself for. You can do this and, you will.

> ''You don't have to solve your
> whole life overnight. And you don't
> have to feel ashamed for being where
> you are. All you have to focus on is
> one small thing you can do today
> to get closer to where you want to be.
> Slowly and lightly, one step at a time.
> You can get there''
> *Daniell Koepke*

When you do, you may think ***oh for the benefit of hindsight.*** But just remember this was your journey. The journey that shaped you for your future.

You will **RISE** and continue your journey but, with a greater knowledge. Knowledge is power. Step into your power.

Huge congratulations to you when you get there.

Sending you love, encouragement and a virtual hug.

Jayne (Holland) xx

Chapter 15 – Claire Zorlutana

"And one day she discovered that she was fierce, and strong, and full of fire, and that not even she could hold herself back because her passion burned brighter than her fears." Mark Anthony, The Beautiful Truth

I sat in my car, staring at the endless queue of traffic in front of me. Feeling anxious, my heart pounding and my pulse racing. I glanced over to the poorly child in the back seat. She sat quietly, her face flushed, running a temperature, but still smiling, like she always does.

For ten years, as a single mum, I had worked so many different jobs. Trying to fit it all in around my kids. Refusing to become another statistic. Nothing was going to get in my way. My three amigos. A team with the strongest bond. No job would ever be more important than my kids.

Yet here I was, driving my poorly child to my parents, 14 miles away, during rush hour. Just so I can show my face at work because I dare not take time off to look after her. Guilt washed over me, and my heart ached.

Sadly, it seems not everyone cares, or understands the importance of family, and how hard it is being a working mum.

An hour late, I arrived in the office, to be met with an icy reception. Not one person spoke to me. A memorable day. One that I will not forget in a hurry. I knew, beyond any doubt, that something had to change. As so often happens fate stepped in!

A few weeks before this incident, I was sitting at home, and put it out to the Universe. I said that I wanted to work for myself and build something around my children, and their needs. I started thinking about what my strengths were and what I was good at. I sat up bleary eyed until 2am constructing a website and designing my business model. I went live the next day!

My strength was always business development and social media. So that was what I based my business on. I wanted to build this up part time, while continuing in my job, where I felt completely undervalued and underpaid.

Unfortunately, this did not go down well with my manager at the time. He saw my new business as competition. After a conversation, he gave me his blessing and I left that day. Anxiety washed over me. Now I really had to stand on my own two feet and make this work. I walked out the door with a heavy heart. But also, with a huge sense of relief.

From now on I will always be there for my children, I will provide for them and create the best future possible. I knew without a shadow of a doubt I would be a success. I had never felt that confident and determined before. I was never going to be dictated to, or bullied out of a job ever again. At that point I stopped giving a shit what people thought of me. Very quickly I was able to take on my first client. I was unstoppable, well so I thought.

I was thoroughly enjoying my newfound freedom. Self-employed and feeling empowered! But, along with many others, I was about to be hit by a huge blow, the hardest of recent times.

March 24th, 2020 will forever be etched on my brain. My daughters 12th birthday and the first day of Lockdown due to Covid 19. I fell into a downward spiral of hopelessness, fear, and anxiety. Like most of the population, I guess. I cried, I got angry, I did not believe this was happening.

I was happily riding the crest of a wave but now I was being dragged out to sea in a Tsunami of fear, doubt, and uncertainty.

Being so recently self-employed, I fell down the rabbit hole of those who did not receive assistance from the government. There was only one thing for it. Go hard or go home Claire! I spent every day working on my business. Networking on Zoom, oh what fun! Overloading my brain with knowledge but maintaining a positive attitude. In a matter of weeks, I started to pick up other clients, slowly but steadily. Who knew that despite a pandemic you could be successful? Me! That's who!

The hardest part of daily life was trying to work my business around the children, now at home all the time. But this was nothing that an early morning or a late night could not fix. It was not unusual for me to be working at 2am and up again at 5.30am. This was not going to beat me!

Ten years earlier the turning point in my life came, when my second husband left me. My children were 7-months, 2 years, and 4 years old. When I found out I had been cheated on by a second husband my world fell apart. It was a very dark time.

I had every intention of driving down the motorway at high speed and driving the car into the central reservation. To make the all the pain go away. Everyone would be better off without me. I could not live with the pain and humiliation a second time.

Someone was watching over me that day, because instead of making that darkest of decisions, I drove to a dark country lane and sat in the car for hours. Crying, sobbing, and letting my heart bleed. Somehow, I remembered that my babies needed their mummy. From that moment on I would be everything to them and fuck that womanizing husband. I rose from the depths of despair and found new strength, by the grace of god.

There is always a point in life where you either give up or you rise. I chose to rise.

A pivotal point came one day when I was out on a shopping trip. I stopped at a charity table, where they were raising money for breast cancer. I was very drawn to a lady on the stall and we chatted. I was feeling like the biggest victim in the world at that point.

She told me her breast cancer story and asked me if I had read a book called The Secret. I was intrigued. Talk about serendipity. I looked across the shopping mall and saw a bookshop, I raced over and found the book!

I read that book in one night. If you have not read it, do it! It's a game changer, and it is magical. I started following the principles of the law of attraction, not in a weird way, in a spiritual way. I believe that you meet the people to teach you lessons. Meeting this lady was an example of this. All this was magically paving the way to my present situation.

I have been pushed so far out of my comfort zone in the last few months. My mantra has been "Say yes to everything". Even if it scares the hell out of you. I cannot tell you many doors this has opened for me. The sense of achievement you feel when you step up and step out of that nice little comfort zone is unreal.

When you work hard only to help line someone else's pocket, it makes you think. I worked my arse off for other people when I was in employment. I was always fully committed and gave a million percent in everything I did.

But at the end of the day no-one really cares about you. You are in effect a number, easily replaced. They do not care if your child is sick, the school is closed or there is an assembly you need to be at. Why be that person, having to put others ahead of your kids and your home commitments?

6 months into my journey I cannot even explain how powerful I feel. I am surrounded by the most inspirational ladies, who wish me only the best. My children understand why mummy works from the kitchen, surrounded by coffee cups, and the odd glass of wine!

They completely understand that I am working to provide a better life, and to afford those little treats that I could not before.

I look back at all the jobs I have ever had. In every single one I have felt discriminated against or bullied. Why did I stay? Because I had to pay my bills, that is why! Going to work even when I was ridiculously ill, in tears, not wanting to be there at all. Knowing I would be belittled or made to feel worthless.

But you know what? Your biggest successes will always come from your biggest fears. Now I choose my hours and my clients. My future is not dictated by some small-minded money driven entrepreneur, only interested in their own success. Why not make your own success? If little old Claire with three children, two marriages and two divorces behind her can make it, then why not you.

I have learned not to let someone else take control of your life. Whether that is an employer, a partner or husband. This is my life, my terms. Those little voices in my head whisper to me sometimes. I hear them saying "Who the hell do you think you are? You can't do this!"

Well guess what! I can. I am thriving. I am not scared anymore. I do not care what other people think. I see people looking at me, checking me out. I am not worried; I am only concerned with going forward and showing the world what I can achieve.

My advice?

Be that person, step out, say yes, be the brave woman you know you are.

You don't need it, but you have my blessing!

Chapter 16 - Lisa Johnson

Love me yesterday and hate me tomorrow but leave me alone today! Lisa Johnson

I am nineteen years old and wishing I had never been born. Attending a writing and drama course, staying at Lumb Bank in Yorkshire, the home Ted Hughes bought after the suicide of his wife, Sylvia Plath. It is whispered amongst us, that this was the house where Sylvia Plath killed herself. That the oven was that oven. It wasn't! The stories we tell each other.

I was miserable. But I seemed to be a flame. A flame that attracted moths. People wanted to be around me. To spend time with me and share my light. Ironically, I felt in eternal night. Nothing I did was good enough. I was not good enough. Why would anyone want to be around me? It didn't make sense.

Staying at Lumb Bank, I felt like I fitted in. This place seemed to suit me. Depression and melancholy seemed to seep out of the walls. Sitting outside, at the back of the house, watching the morning mist roll in. I smoked cigarettes, thinking about how magical, how peaceful it would be if I could just turn out the light. If this last blissful, drawn out toke on a cigarette could be my last taste of anything. If I could simply cease to exist right at that moment. How would that be?

I was in the barn completing a workshop with Suzie, who I was in awe of. She had worked with Harold Pinter. Attended the prestigious Jacques Lecoq theatre school in Paris. But more than that. She seemed to have her shit together. And she saw me. She saw the frightened, fragile girl I was. She saw into my soul and told me "Things do get better".

I became very ill while I was there, and she was the first person to tell me that sometimes you need to listen to your body. You must let your body heal. This was a revelation. I had been taught "No weakness, no illness. Do not be weak. Do not EVER be weak'. Ironically at the time I believed that I a weak, broken, fragile doll. Of no value to anyone.

I was standing there, waiting my turn, next to wear the mask. The instruction was simple. Wear the mask and walk around the room. I saw myself wearing the mask. Floating round the room, swirling, making tai chi moves, dancing. An elegant version of myself, the me I wanted to be.

Behind the mask, I would be free, I thought. Free from me. Excitedly I put the mask on my face and tied it at the back. I opened my eyes. Something came over me. I froze. I looked at the people in the room and I wanted to cry. I thought that behind the mask I would finally be myself. But I felt naked. I wanted to cry or hide. To scream "Stop fucking looking at me". With my face hidden I felt exposed, as though my soul had been laid bare. There was nowhere to hide. Everything I hated was on view.

I managed to move. My heavy legs and my body followed. Time stood still and it was torture. I was burning inside. Suzie looked at me and said, "You're an enigma". She called me Princess Diana and Marilyn Monroe. "One-minute shy and introverted, begging people not to look at you. The next brazen and screaming to be seen, to be given attention. To be desired". An introverted extrovert.

I did not understand what she meant. It was another stick to beat myself with.

The quote at the top of the first page is my mantra for life. As soon as I could pick up a pen, I wrote. I wrote to fill a void inside me. As a child, I had learned that love was conditional. It was not free. It had to be earned. If you pissed off the people you loved, there would be punishment. Or days of silence. I learned to be amenable. To please and seek approval through my actions. Measuring my worth by the approval of others.

I am deeply affected by the emotions of others. I would hide in my room and write about my woes. But with the companionship of my very best friend. Music. Music spoke to parts of me that I could not reach. I would dance into a trance and forget the world outside of the walls that confined me.

The introverted extrovert again. Not wanting to be seen, hiding in my safe and happy place while still longing for approval. Looking for the love we all yearn for.

That time in Lumb Bank had a profound effect on me. To this day I can recall the week in minute detail. It taught me that we never see what others see. I hated myself. I felt unloved. But other people saw something different.

When I was very young, my mother would say I was obsessed with men. That I would be pregnant by the time I was 14. She said it a lot. And low and behold at 15, I missed my period. I was terrified. Was I having sex? Yes. Awkward, painful intercourse experienced as a minor who was ill equipped for coping with the emotions that having sex brings. Never mind pregnancy. Terrified, in my childhood bathroom with no lock on the door, I did a pregnancy test. As the two lines turned blue the world shifted out of focus. I sank to the floor in despair.

I prayed for a different result. Please do not let my mother be right. My partner knocked on the door. As terrified as I was. We left the house. To walk and talk, away from the oppression in my home and two sisters who despised me.

We fled to the alley at the end of the road, with me in tears. That gave way to fits of hysterical laughter as I handed the pee stick to the boy. Also a child, not even my boyfriend anymore. We loved each other, but the relationship was toxic. I had held hands with another boy the weekend before and dreamt of another life. I was so naive and inexperienced.

Pregnant at 15. Not a fucking clue about sex. I was shy and awkward. One of the last girls in my class to kiss anyone. In fact, this boy, the "father" of this blip inside me, had humiliated me in front of the whole school a few years earlier, because I wouldn't kiss him. I had never kissed anyone. He caused me pain and bullying from other boys about how I walked and being frigid. But now here I was. Pregnant with his child and fucking terrified.

I watched the colour drain from his face. His home life wasn't a piece of cake either. He was more terrified than me. We were young. We were both fucked up beyond measure and we did not have a clue. The only option was no option at all. To terminate. I phoned the doctor for the first time in my life and asked for an appointment.

He was old. His hands were cold and he felt my tummy. There was no discussion. He was sure that termination was the right thing. He pressed hard on my stomach and said "Yes, you are pregnant but if you are lucky you will miscarry. Most women do".

We went to the appointment hand in hand. Back together again through fear and circumstance. They took us in a little room and told me to remove my trousers. I had no idea what was going on. She was speaking, but all I could think about was being naked from the waist down. I climbed on the bed and shivered as she inserted a wand inside me.

There on the screen was a tiny blip of nothingness. My heart lurched as she pointed out the heartbeat and I saw this baby that was mine.

Did I change my mind? No.
Did it fucking kill me? Yes, almost.
Part of me died that day when that bloody little blip escaped into a cardboard potty.

I had had sex with this boy to please him. It hurt and I bled and never wanted to do it again. But I did because I wanted to please him. For him to love me. Even though I was unloveable.

We walked away from that place. When I pulled up my pants, with sticky, cold gel clinging to my vagina and legs. I cried for the baby I had lost. I cried for myself and I cried for him.

I aborted my baby on 14 January 2000. Because I was afraid. Afraid of my parents. But also, out of spite. Because of my mother. Fuck her. Fuck her for being right.

Standing in that barn in Lumb Bank 4 years later. I was still punishing myself for having an abortion. I hated myself. I used words like murderer, and I was filled with unimaginable shame. The story in my head went like this, my parents, my family did not love me. Unless I was good. Unless I did everything to make them happy. My two sisters called me Lapdog Lisa and it is only recently I can say that name without pain.

Who else would love me now? I did not deserve it. I deserved to die.

The misery of that 15-year-old girl's trauma led me down a path of destruction.

I harmed myself with cigarettes and alcohol. I drank till I blacked out. I am only here due to the kindness and love of some I encountered along the way. Those who saw my light when all I saw was darkness.

I would love to share their names. Share their impact they made on me. Show you their imprints on my heart. But that would embarrass them, and many of them are no longer in my life. Maintaining friendships was impossible for a unloveable, self-destructive girl with attachment issues.

Why did I start my story with Lumb bank?
Well, it is where I finally realised I had come apart at the seams and needed help. Again because of a man... maybe my mother was right!

I had just broken up with a man who I believed was the love of my life. He saw me. He saw my darkness and he saw my light and he loved me. He tried to make me feel loved. After the pregnancy and termination. After that I had not been with another man. I had not had sex. It terrified me and I never enjoyed it anyway.

Then I met this man.

He was 23. I was 18. He had a car and a job. He seemed like he had his shit together, but it was an illusion. He loved cocaine and cannabis and he had demons. But he worshipped me. He set me high on a pedestal.

Created an image that was impossible to live up to. One that I didn't feel worthy of. He taught me the joy of making love. The carnality of fucking and kinky sex. I did not believe I deserved him, but I worshipped him back. I put him on a pedestal too. I would have done anything he wanted. Anything. But I needed to know that he would stay. I tested him, time and again. Pushing his buttons to see if he would leave.

I convinced myself that it would be best if he left. When he stayed, I didn't know what to do.

In a drunken stupor, I cheated on him. Not once but twice. I slept with someone else. I was drunk. I was in a foreign country and too scared to say no. This strange man, whose name I don't remember, strangled me while he fucked me and when it was over, he kissed me on the forehead, and I walked back to my apartment in a daze.

Full of shame again, a fuck up who had cheated on the only person who had ever shown her love. After that I kissed his brother in another drunken dark haze.

The next day was his birthday and he cooked us steaks and we made love on the floor while I wept. I wanted him to hate me. The way I hated myself. The way my family hated me. I ended the relationship and broke his heart. He didn't know it, but I broke my own heart too. The heartbreak from losing him brought me to the lowest point of my life.

I knew I needed help. I wanted to win him back, I believed that with his love and forgiveness I could learn to forgive myself. I sought help from a counsellor. What a shit show that was. I poured my heart out. From childhood to young adult. Every shitty detail.

And what did she do? She sat and cried.

She cried for what I'd been through. I looked at her in disbelief, shocked and a little afraid. Was my life that bad? Was my life worse than I realised? So bad in fact that this lady would sit and cry about it?

I never went back to that counsellor. I vowed never to see one again. But it started something beautiful. A relationship with myself and the discovery of my spirituality. Although I would go on to fuck up again, often. And although I would continue to punish myself for the mistakes I made and have shared with you. That day in the counsellor's office started my journey of self-development.

I buried myself in books, attended courses and learned more about spirituality and how it had always been an amazing and important part of my life. I just had not realised it.

What about now?

I am the woo-woo queen of an amazing business. I help women find their light, their strength, and their power alongside another amazing, strong woman. We have come together to share our experiences and the tools we have used to help ourselves. It is everything that I needed back then. When I thought I was wicked and broken, I wasn't. I was just HURT and HEALING. Hurt people, hurt people. We have a responsibility to do the work and heal ourselves.

So much has changed. At last I have a great relationship with my family and my sisters. I adore them and am grateful to have them in my life. We are honest with each other. I have a voice and I goddamn use it. There is mutual respect. I demand it.

I cannot deny there have been challenges in my life. They did not just magically disappear when I learned to own my shit and discovered self-development. That's not how life works. I am challenged daily.

The universe throws shit at me all the time. But I am no longer a VICTIM. I take responsibility for my life and my actions. As a child I sought to please everyone. I craved approval. That was not my fault, but as an adult it is my RESPONSIBILITY to own that shit and overcome it.

I am the only person in charge of my behaviour. I will never again blame others for my actions and my choices. I own my shit. The good and the bad. Without everything I have been through I would not be here.

I would not be able to help other women see their fucking power and their light. I did the best I could. I also know that so did my parents. So did my sisters. Once I stood up for myself, found my voice, I was able to stand in my power. Now I have a great relationship with all of them.

Getting from there to here was not easy. It's been challenging facing myself and owning my shit, but you know what? It has it been worth it and now I get to help others.

I was not lost, I was not broken. I was not evil. I was a very mixed up little girl who did the best she could at the time. I do not regret anything I went through or how I dealt with it. It has taken me a long time to be able to say that. I no longer feel shame.

Did I fuck up? Yes.

Did I hurt people along the way? Yes. But the person I hurt the most was me.

Every time I said yes when I meant NO.

Every time I did something I did not want to do.

But I have forgiven myself. I did the best that I could. I am sorry I hurt the people that I did. But I no longer feel ashamed. I am not that person anymore. I am no longer a prisoner of my past. I no longer have a victim mentality.

I own My shit.

I own my life and I stand in my POWER.
If I make a mistake, it is my mistake, and I learn from it.
Do not let anyone make you feel bad for something you did when you didn't know better.
Do not wear other people's shame for them.
You are amazing and you have done the best you can.
You can heal from anything. It won't always be easy, but you can. If you have the will and the mindset.

Today, my life is spent helping other women to find their passion and their power. I am passionate about helping them learn to own their past. To own it, release it and no longer be a prisoner of it. To forgive their younger selves and be grateful that the lessons made them who they are today.

What is my quote now? I have two;
If you don't love the life you live, create a life you love.

In the silent stillness I found my voice, and I found that I could ROAR.

You are in charge of your life. No one else.
Do not give your power to others.
Do not dim your light to make others feel better.

You are a goddamn Goddess and you were meant to shine! You came here with a gift to share with the world. If you are not sharing it right now, it's time you did.

I hope my story and the sister stories in this book help you to find your roar. To find your passion and your purpose to share with the world.

Hiding your light and pretending to be someone you are not robs the world of your unique magic.

There is only one of you and thank goodness for that!

You are truly unique and amazing.

Chapter 17 – Kerrie Patterson

Copyright The Inner Feminine Collective 2020

"Find the courage to step into your flamingo, because you're worth so much more than you think you are"
Kerrie Patterson

This is my story of finding my own inner flamingo.

As I sat at my desk crying, and repeating to myself 'I can't cope', I had no idea just how much my life was about to change. With a successful career as a qualified Probation Officer, for fifteen years. I had helped lots of people to move on with their lives. I had trained staff nationally to deliver accredited programmes. I had been promoted to oversee staff development and was enjoying my part time hours.

So what was the matter with me? Surely things were not that bad? Yes, I was tired, and as a busy mum with two young boys, life could be very stressful. But to be crying like this? It just did not make sense to me.

When the Doctor told me that I was completely burnt out and suffering from work related stress, it was a shock. I thought that maybe I needed a short rest from work, but to be signed off for at least 4 weeks with immediate effect, was not what I expected. I worked hard and I had annual leave that I could use. But taking time off what not what I did.

Then, as I began to reflect on the last few months, I realised that this had been building up for a long time. I had been struggling to process and retain new information for a while. And, following the recent privatisation of the service, there had been huge changes in a very short time.

I started to worry that something was seriously wrong with me. Maybe I needed a brain scan or memory test. Some days were so bad that I could barely open my emails, I just sat staring at the screen for hours. My home life was starting to be adversely affected. I was irritable and tearful at the slightest thing.

I knew that I would have to make serious changes in my life, but I just did not think I had it in me. My mind was exhausted. I could barely make it out of the house or even my bed, some days.

Once I finally accepted the need to take time to rest, my mind slowly came back into focus. I was still struggling with thoughts and worries about my future, but slowly this started to ease. I found it really helpful to throw myself into creative projects. I never have considered myself a creative person but the calm of painting a piece of furniture, really calmed me, and began the process of healing.

I began to wonder if there was maybe more to life than sitting in an office. I started to upcycle vintage furniture for friends and family. The sheer joy of transforming something neglected, into a beautiful piece again, made my heart sing. It gave me a reason to get up in the morning and calmed my tired mind. I made the decision there and then that I was not going back. Whatever I had to do, to make up the shortfall in income, I would make it work.

After an emotionally tough period, I eventually secured my redundancy pay. It felt bittersweet to give up a career which I had invested so much of myself and some days I felt so angry. So, I did something positive. Just for me. I used part of the payment to build a workshop in my garden.

A space for me alone and my potential new business. I kitted it out with electricity, lighting, a compressor stapler, and lots of fabrics. I found a new passion, a love of colours and textures.
I realised that I had been a creative person all along. It was not something that I believed, after recognising at school that I did not have a talent for drawing or painting.

However, I now discovered that I did have an amazing, and creative, talent for interiors and colour matching. Feeling inspired, I trained to be an upholsterer. The sense of achievement when I had finished my first chair, was so uplifting! I learned new skills. Not only how to strip back an old armchair, but how to put it back together again. In the process, I felt like I was also putting myself back together again, piece by piece. I even learnt to sew. And to put together eclectic pieces of fabric into a modern, bright patchwork design.

I felt like I was finally becoming the true me, a person with energy, enthusiasm, and passion. I gained the confidence to do commission pieces and taught myself how to make cushions. At last, I felt truly at peace, sitting at a sewing machine in my workshop, music blasting.

I dipped my toe into the business world, but I realised that I still thought of myself as an ex-probation officer. I just didn't see how my 'little business' could ever make enough money. I constantly worried about having to return to an office, just so we could pay the mortgage.

Adding to the fear, my husband had also had a huge career change, from civil servant to business owner. What if this business did not make enough money? We had two children to support and provide for. We had gone from two guaranteed monthly wages to two new businesses, with unpredictable futures. It was an incredibly tough time and we were struggling to manage.

My demons returned in full force, telling me that my skills were not good enough, I wasn't good enough. I felt low and deflated. And then, that I walked into a women's networking meeting which would change everything.

I like to think that things happen for a reason and that the right people come to us just when we need them. To prove my point, at this first network meeting, I met the most inspirational woman.

There were lots of women who inspired me but there was something about this person, that just had me in awe. Her confidence, knowledge, and wisdom as she spoke, made any subject sound interesting and inspiring. I had an intuitive feeling right then, that I would somehow work with this amazing woman. I was right.

Fast forward a few months and she gifted me the most incredible opportunity I think I have ever experienced. The chance for her to be my mentor on a 12-month programme, which would not only build me back up, but also my business. I could not believe that she had sensed an ability and talent in me that I didn't even recognise in myself.

Fast forward to today and I am finally embracing who I am and what I can offer to the world. Through my mentorship journey of self-development, I have finally found my calling and I am embracing it with fully. In another lightbulb moment, I realised that I was an empath, which explained my passion to help and support others.

It led me down a different path, guiding me to support women who have been made to feel small through bullying, just as I was. I finally saw that my lack of confidence and self-worth stemmed from incidents of bullying as a child, and also as an adult.

The nasty looks and comments intended to put me down, to humiliate me. People who felt that they could take advantage of my placid nature, causing my already limited self-worth, to plummet even further.

I decided that enough was enough. I was going to step into my courage and start to share my story.

I would use my personal experience combined with the skills from my career, to support other women through online programmes. I am now doing exactly that and actively embracing my creativity.

Fusing it into my programmes. I help women to not only transform a piece of furniture, but to transform themselves in the process with tried and tested techniques. It is my passion and my dream. I created my Stand Tall Academy. With a flamingo as my icon.

I encourage and empower women to stand tall, like me!

So why am I sharing this with you? Because I want you to be able to step into your own flamingo.

We all have it within us. That gut feeling, our 'inner flamingo' desperate to get out and stand tall. Maybe we have trapped it inside. Because of our past experiences, our self-doubt.

But we need to learn to listen. Because when it speaks, it is telling us that we need to change.

No need to be scared. Harness the fear to drive you forward.

You will never know unless you take that first step. If this bullied, self-conscious mum of two could take that step, make that change, then anyone can. You owe it to yourself and the world.

Because you are amazing.

You just may not realise it yet.
Be brave, say yes to every opportunity and share your story with the world.

Trust me, you will feel amazing.

Chapter 18 – Wendy Concannon

You've always had the power my dear, you just had to learn it for yourself – the Wizard of Oz.

I have always had the power. I know that now. But after years of burying my dreams, keeping quiet instead of speaking up, and ignoring my power, I realise that life has been teaching me some incredible lessons. Waiting for me to discover the power of my voice, and breathe life into all my desires, with courage, knowing my true value and my worth.

I am unsure of how or when my limiting beliefs started. But I do remember being incredibly shy at primary school. I never liked to answer questions in class and hated raising my hand to do so. I was convinced that if I knew the answer, then it must be wrong. So, I kept quiet. I would shrink into my chair at question time, terrified of being seen and asked to read from a book, or give an answer to a question. Academically, I was average, but I excelled in lacking in self-belief, courage, confidence, and conviction.

The allocation of roles for the school play would cause every cell in my body to vibrate, on high alert, in a panic that I might be selected. The teacher was determined to give *every* child an acting role. Begrudgingly I accepted the part of, a buffalo! A buffalo! I was a tiny six-year-old, incredibly thin, playing a buffalo in the school nativity. A buffalo in a nativity? I really hated being weighed down by the expectation to perform.

In another school play I played the part of a princess. Oh! How I hated that, even more. For some, a dream role, but not for me. Having to speak, move, act and convey emotions on stage, was terrifying. Every ounce of me did not want to do it. I felt awkward and embarrassed. Not good enough. I kept trying to hide my face throughout the performance.

Throughout primary school I was bullied. For being skinny, for having big lips and big eyes. My parents divorced when I was 10 years old, and the school kids found another excuse to attack me. Verbally and physically. I never knew how to defend myself or fight back. I just accepted what was given. I spoke to my parents about the bullying, and my mum would have meetings with the headteacher to bring the bullies to justice. I appreciated this, but it did not improve the situation.

My end of year school reports described me as a dreamer. My imagination carried me away to far off places, much to the dismay of the teachers. I loved moments of stillness, being alone and daydreaming, but at school this was not allowed, and I was made to feel bad for losing myself in thought.

Senior school brought some relief, but I continued feeling undeserving and unheard. Despite that, I got through my GCSE's in 1989 with grades good enough to grant me a place in college.

Although I struggled to speak up and be heard in class, I was ambitious and desperate to achieve! But I still lacked self-belief and confidence. I was told that people from the north cannot be successful and I allowed those words to dampen the fire within me. I downgraded my hopes, I changed my plans and got a job in an office after three years at college.

It was never in my plans to be a secretary, but here I was, aged 19, living alone in London, making a living doing a job that barely paid my bills. My first full time job. But to maintain a basic decent standard of living, I had to take on a part time job in a bar as well. Two years working full-time, and part time wore me down. I returned home to the north-east of England, my ambition and dreams boxed and buried, feeling deflated and defeated.

I later developed an interest in mental wellbeing. I went back to education to study for the qualifications I needed to obtain a degree in Psychology. My inner voice was whispering to me to dig up those dreams and bring them to life.

I was married with one daughter and another on the way. Finding childcare was difficult with two children, and we could not afford putting both into nursery, especially as my husband was the only one earning. I buried another goal and became a stay at home mum for the next four years. This was a wonderful luxury and I thoroughly enjoyed it, but I knew I needed to do more. I was constantly reminded that I had not reached my potential or fulfilled my dreams. I felt frustrated.

In October 2001, with both girls now at school, I began working weekends in a pharmacy as a dispenser. I enjoyed helping people improve their health but still felt something was missing. So, I looked into more study. Health and wellbeing were very important to me and I wanted to add to my ever-growing skills.

In 2002 I trained to become a fitness instructor. I had always enjoyed keeping fit and I was desperate to overcome my shyness, and fear of being seen. I dipped my toe into personal development. I had been attending fitness classes for years and I distinctly remember thinking 'I could do this. I could teach a class. Enough of being shy Wendy. Let's face this fear!'

The course was incredible. I enjoyed learning as an adult much more than I did as a child or adolescent. I was finally doing something I loved and that I could do with passion. My confidence grew and I was overjoyed when I passed my course with flying colours. I took a job in the local leisure centre.

For two years, 2002 – 2004, I enjoyed working as a fitness instructor, teaching a variety of fitness classes, as well as working part time at the Pharmacy. The hours I worked fitted around school times, and my husband's work and it meant I was earning a full-time wage. I felt like I was contributing. I was working in health and wellbeing and I loved it.

It was incredible coaching people on healthy lifestyle choices, taking a variety of classes and seeing others improve their health. It was hard work, managing two jobs and home life.

But I was so proud I had worked on my fear of being seen and heard. Little did I know that I had not really put all those demons to bed.

For a long time, I sought advice from others. I often felt indecisive, not trusting my own decisions. Feeling that other's opinions were more valid than my own. I would often ask 'What should I do?'.

One of those times was in 2004 when I applied for, and successfully gained, a full-time job as an Assistant Manager at the pharmacy. I felt like I should relish the opportunity to pursue this career, but it meant having to quit the fitness instructor job I loved, as I physically could not do both.

A tough decision as I wanted to just have one job to focus on, but, being a fitness instructor full-time was impossible. Being a manager was what I thought I 'should' do.

So, I jumped in. It was a steady job with a salary, and I progressed through the ranks and become a Store Manager.

For a long time, I loved the job, I was grateful for it and pleased I had embarked on a career in management, despite it not being in my original plans. I appreciated the advice and support of friends and family who had guided me at that time.

As the years passed, I began to feel stressed and unfulfilled. Something did not quite fit. I felt deep within, that I needed to be doing something else, but I was not sure what exactly. I now know that this was my inner guide nudging me, but I chose not to listen at that time.

I was once on a training course and asked what I wanted for my future. "I want to be a coach" I replied. Wow, I said it! I actually declared out loud what I wanted. I was surprised to hear those words come out of my mouth. It was as if my inner guide had spoken the words on my behalf.

I was visualising myself delivering coaching sessions to a group of women and it felt good. There were elements of my current job I loved but others I did not. The role and I did not vibrate on the same frequency. I had had some success but could not maintain it. I did not feel fulfilled anymore.

I was incredibly stressed, personally, and professionally. Barely eating, not sleeping, and travelling a lot. Basically, I was falling apart. My performance at work was falling short. I was not myself. I was at breaking point.

During a week of annual leave, I was experiencing high levels of anxiety even though I was away from work. I saw that it was seriously impacting my health, and something had to give. I rang my line-manager and declared I was stepping down. I had to relieve myself of at least one of the stressors in my life and it was the right decision to make. This was a decision I made alone.

I did not consult anyone in the process. My intuition knew with absolute certainty that I had do make this happen. I was not prepared to be talked out of it.

My inner guide had been whispering to me all along. Telling me something was not right. When I did not listen, the voice became louder. When I ignored it, it nudged me. Then, finally it was yelling, and shaking me to take action!

That was when I took notice. When I felt like I was falling apart, that is when I realised, I had to listen.

Within weeks of quitting the relief I felt was immense. Allowing me to focus on my homelife and start to piece myself back together. With hindsight, I can see clearly how much of a wreck I had become. It was spring 2014 and by September, I had begun my journey of self-care.

Nourishing my body with good food, I had re-joined the gym and was lifting weights several times a week. I was reading again, becoming more focused, grounded and more aligned with myself.

I cut out alcohol massively. During my years as a retail manager I would have two to three glasses of wine most evenings, to help me decompress from everything going on. But with my new focus on health and wellbeing, I no longer wanted to reach for the pinot grigio.

I began reading more books on mental wellbeing, emotional grit, and personal development. I was listening to my inner guide and it felt good.

I still had a long way to go on my journey. My job as a dispenser was not stressful, and I was working on myself.

But still not fully embracing the whispers in my ear. Between 2015 and 2018 I put myself through extreme training and diet regimes as I became a body-building athlete.

Competing on stage and winning trophies. It was intense. I loved it and I let my light shine on that stage. I committed whole-heartedly and pushed myself hard. As an athlete, its essential. You have to fully commit to the demand of the sport.

Despite professional stress no longer being part of my life, personally, I still was not in a good place. Powerful emotions, a magnitude of pain, sorrow, and despair. On reflection training hard for hours and hours was a way of escaping what I was feeling inside. A coping mechanism. Many bodybuilders refer to the gym as their sanctuary, a place of escape and its true. I found myself escaping to the gym for hours at a time.

My personal development journey had revealed to me how I was a people pleaser. I realised that I was forever doing what others wanted, sacrificing my own plans, goals, and dreams. It was then that I sought counselling. The sessions were powerful and many of the issues I had carried with me throughout my adult life were laid to rest. I began to use my voice. I found my power, and my courage. I spoke what was in my heart. I forgave those who had caused me pain. I forgave myself. An incredible release!

I told that 10-year-old girl inside me, who dreamed of better days, that she has the power to be whoever and whatever she wants to be. Her voice is worthy of being heard.

Being so grateful for the counselling sessions I received reminded me of my desire to help others be the best version of themselves.

I heard my inner guide sigh with relief that I was finally tuning in to what she had been telling me for so long.
I began training to become a Life Coach. Taking every opportunity to study, fitting it around work and preparing for my final competition in bodybuilding of the 2018 season. The course was intense and fast paced. Sleep was minimal but I was determined to grow in exponential ways and finally step into the dream I had kept buried.

By late summer of that year, with the competition behind me, I threw myself into personal growth. I had finished my counselling sessions and I was done with being comfortable. I knew I had a lot more to give. By October I had enrolled on a course to become a counsellor.

It is now 2020 and I am qualified as a Life Coach, NLP Practitioner and Meditation Practitioner and have completed two years of Counselling studies. Devoting time for personal growth, achieving these qualifications, equipping myself with new skills feels incredible.

Qualifications alone were not enough though. I still had not truly stepped up. I felt unable to step into the working world as a coach. All that study, all those skills and qualifications, and here I was in March 2020 feeling like an imposter if I step into the arena.

I was in comparison mode and holding myself back, getting in my own way. I was afraid; to take the next step, to declare "I am a Life Coach", to launch a business. Heck, I didn't even know *how* to set up a business. Even afraid to ask for help. That little girl too frightened to speak up, returned.

Then, as so often happens, the universe aligned everything perfectly. Just as I was thinking about finding myself a coach, I stumbled upon another coach on an online networking group , who was also brand new on her journey, looking for clients to practice her skills on, for free, in return for testimonials.

It was a golden opportunity. I declared my interest and revealed to her my plans. We talked about what was holding me back worked together, setting goals for me to achieve each week.

The first week I as to contact a business strategist that I knew. Sara is incredible. I had known her via Facebook for about year. If anyone could help me develop a business from concept to launch, it was Sara. Everything in my life had led me to this exact moment. Now was my time. With weekly zoom calls with both coaches I finally stepped into my power.

I felt vulnerable reaching out and asking for support from others in the field. Announcing to friends and family that I was setting up a coaching business was incredibly daunting. But I faced the fear, squashed that inner, critical, self-sabotaging voice and I declared my vision out loud.
I waited for the responses that I had played out in my head such as, 'Really? Can you make money from it?' 'Who uses or needs a coach?' and the worst one 'What can you coach people on?' I did not receive any of those responses. Guess who had been overthinking and preparing for the worse case scenario? Me!

Here I am, confident and courageous. Wendy Concannon, Life Coach. With my own business, Empowered Women Coaching. My life is blissful, joyful, and abundant. Deeply in love with my hubby, our children are grown and flourishing, my family are healthy, and I am truly blessed and grateful.

I sense my inner guide doing a happy dance, I feel the rhythm of her dance as I embrace this new chapter. I know that I belong in this space. I have waited for years. I have an abundance of experience and skills. Gathered while I was digging around to find the courage to finally be me. This, along with those qualifications, demonstrate that I can and do, own my place in the coaching arena.

This is not the entire story of Wendy Concannon. It is the story of how I felt powerless to speak up, crazy for dreaming big, and how, due to my lack of self-belief, I held myself back. It is the story of how life is always whispering to you. Your dreams were given to you to be fulfilled. Go out there and bring them to life.

What an incredible journey I have been on. I am enjoying each moment, and I am excited for what is to come.
There are many lessons I have learned. Here are some I want to share with you:

The power lies within you. You have always had the power, you just had to learn it for yourself.

Trust your inner guide. Life will whisper to you. When you don't listen, the voice will become louder and louder. Listen and trust your inner guide, that gut instinct is your internal sat nav.

If nothing changes, nothing changes.

The universe always gives you what you have the courage to ask for. But be prepared to grow in incredible ways first. Never stop investing in you and your growth.

Chapter 19 – Vivienne Edgecombe

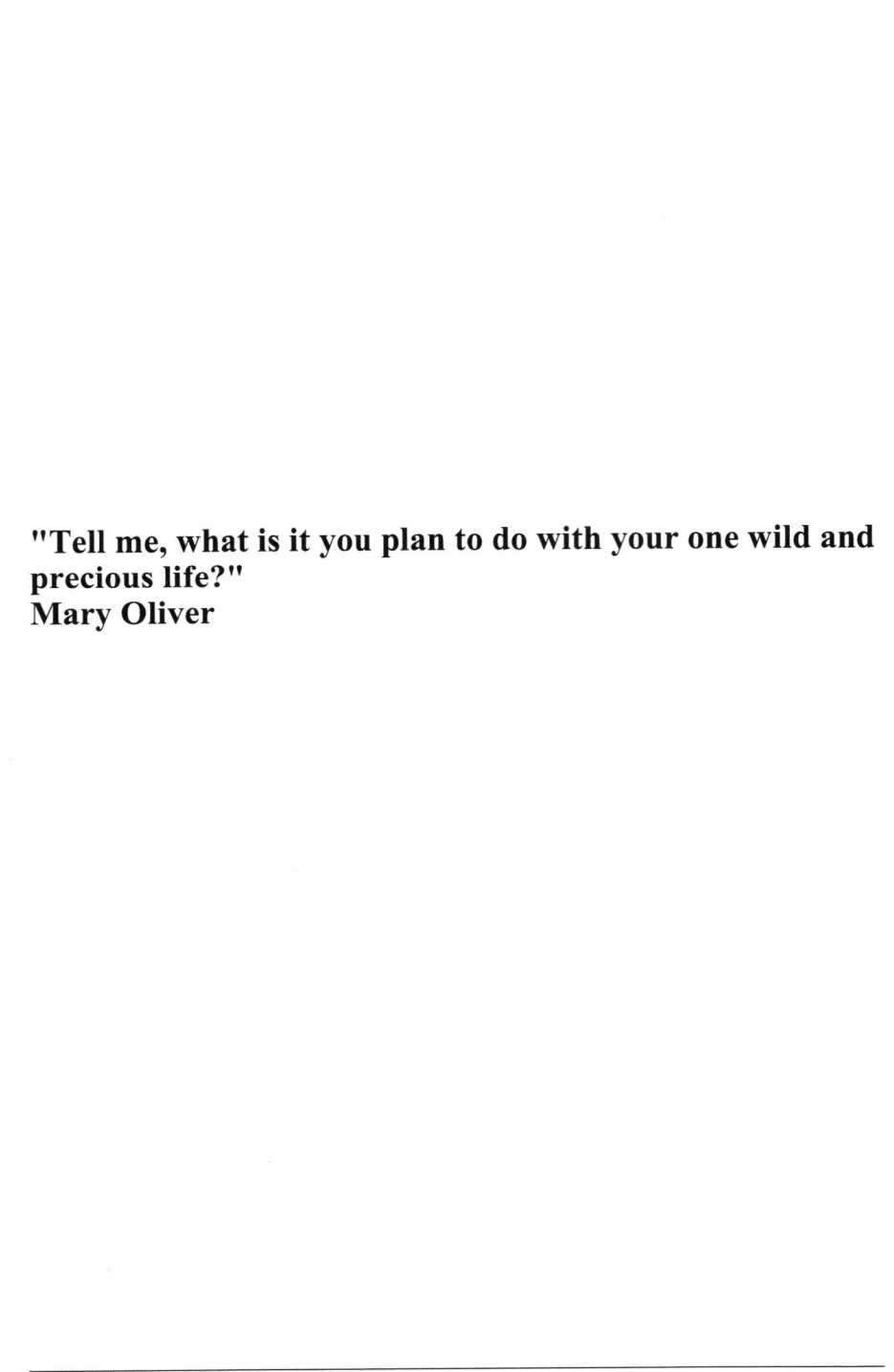

"Tell me, what is it you plan to do with your one wild and precious life?"
Mary Oliver

A Life Unexpected

While on the surface, what follows might seem like a story for those who wanted children and couldn't or didn't have them, there's something in here for every human being whose life hasn't turned out how they thought it would. It speaks to the completeness of us and the infinite potential we all have to see life fresh in each moment.

You see, for a large chunk of my 30s, I was caught in a trap that, try as I might, I could not find a way out of. My life had taken an unexpected turn, and I was struggling to come to terms with the idea that I would not have children.

I thought, and believed without question, that without children my life would be 'second-rate' and that I was therefore doomed to never be quite happy or quite fulfilled. This looked completely real to me, and this view of life seemed reinforced by almost everyone I spoke to and everything I saw and read. No one told me I could just be happy. It seemed like a huge problem to me, and everyone I spoke to seemed to agree.

I had two very vivid versions of the future mapped out. The one I could not have, complete with picket fence, sunlit and rose tinted, with a husband and two children. And the one I thought I was headed for, lonely and grey with a great gaping hole of sadness in it.

This might sound familiar to you, if you wanted children but did not have them, or if you are coming to the end of the 'trying to conceive' road with no baby in sight. People's efforts to help are generally well-intentioned but misguided, given that they are all operating from the same misunderstanding that had me caught in that trap for so long.

They try to make us feel better by telling us about all the things we will be able to do if we don't have children (think of the money you'll save!), they tell us to move on and let it go, or conversely, not to give up, because only by having children could we possibly be fulfilled, complete, happy.

And it all looks so real. It truly seemed to me that I was destined for a lesser life without children. I remember thinking "Surely not. Surely it can't be true that my life will inevitably be less rich and less fulfilled, just because I don't have children. Surely that's not a rule of the Universe". It sure seemed true, but the wisdom in me somehow did not accept it.

Then one day, I experienced a moment of deep and lasting change. I had an insight that opened the door to a whole new way of seeing my life.

I realised in that moment, that the futures I was envisaging weren't real. They were made up. Both of them, even the rose-tinted one. The sadness I felt, when I felt it, was a result of experiencing the made-up grey future here and now. Not a result of any truth about what my future would be like. Neither of them was the *actual* future I would have. Because *I cannot tell the future.*

That threw everything wide open for me. My future no longer seemed fixed and I no longer dwelled on what my life would be like without children, because it seemed a bit silly to get so tied up in something so completely imaginary. It just did not seem relevant to do that anymore, and as a result, rafts of painful, tortured thinking just fell away without me having to do anything at all. I spent much more of my time in the 'here and now', rather than projecting myself off into some imagined painful future.

The shift was seismic and liberating. But there was more to come. I carried on with my life, feeling much freer, but with that realisation compartmentalised. In other aspects of my life I still felt constrained and kept bumping into sharp corners, particularly in my relationships and my work.

Perhaps the biggest sticking point, with the most ripple effects, was that I still felt like I needed some purpose, or some way to 'make up for' not having children, because it wasn't enough just to be me. I was constantly searching for 'my why' or 'my purpose' and did not seem able to find it, no matter how hard I looked.

A couple of years later, I had moved to London with my partner, and lived through some interesting but often uncomfortably bumpy times. I was deep into self-development, believing that if I could master all these techniques to get rid of all my limiting beliefs, then the sky would be the limit for me and for all my future coaching clients.

The problem was, it seemed like every time I got rid of one belief, another one would pop up in its place. Or the same one would come back in another form. A bit like a never-ending game of whack-a-mole. For all the 'work' on purpose, all the finding my 'why', nothing really settled into my bones and felt like it was what I was 'meant' to be doing. What I really wanted, but thought was just a 'nice idea', was to move to France and write a book.

That did not seem purposeful enough though. And I wasn't even sure what the book would be about! So, I carried on searching for the thing that would make me worthy of existence given that I had not had children.

In 2009, on yet another self-development course, I was introduced to an understanding that would rock my world, gently but oh-so-firmly. It made sense of what had happened when I had that insight several years before, and why I had felt so stuck for so long. It showed me why I hadn't been able to 'find my purpose', why I was still struggling to be at peace with my feelings around not having children, and still feeling at the mercy of so many things and people in my life. It is hard to put into words what I was shown, but here's my best attempt.

Firstly, I saw that whether or not you have children has **nothing whatsoever** to do with your ability to find happiness, fulfilment or contentment in this life.

Zero percent.

Nothing.

Thought is the creator of your entire experience of life. And even when you *think* that you aren't whole, complete or fulfilled, *you already are all those things.* I saw how one minute I was perfectly content and the next I would be crying into my pillow, and nothing had changed but my thinking. I looked around me and saw people with and without children who were not happy. I saw people with and without children who were happy, and people with and without children who were sometimes happy and sometimes miserable. I saw their (and my) thinking playing out in every moment. It was like everyone was walking around with thought-bubbles floating above their heads.

Seeing that for myself freed me (mostly) from being at the mercy of my thinking. I became largely unafraid of what was going on in my head, because I was no longer obliged to believe it, no matter how real it seemed. My moods evened out, I was less judgemental, relationships softened and deepened, and work became easier and less stressful. Life seemed gentler.

Secondly, I saw that there is nothing you need to do, or be, or have, that could make you worthy of your place in this world. You are an expression of life in action. You were born worthy, and the only thing stopping you from realising that, *is the thought that you are not*. The result of this realisation was that I stopped looking for 'a purpose' and instead, moved to France just like I'd always dreamed of, and wrote two books (with a third on the way).

Thirdly, and perhaps most importantly, there is *nothing* that could fulfil you, make you 'more whole' or complete; *you are already complete*. You came into this world a perfect, ordinary miracle of nature, and nothing of the essence of that miracle has been taken from you since then – how could it be? The only thing stopping you from realising that you are already complete, *is the thought that you are not*.

As a result of realising this for myself, I finally found true peace about not having children. It no longer defines me in any way. The fact that I don't have children is not a particular feature in my life, apart from when I'm writing about it or sharing for the purpose of helping others to come to peace with their circumstances. I don't feel the need to give myself a label of childless or child free or any other 'child-related' label. Why would I, when whether or not I have children has nothing to do with my value or identity in the world?

This has been the biggest gift I could have been given; it's an understanding of the nature of Thought and the nature of Life, that has given me a foundation, that is so rock solid, I no longer have to be scared of what the future holds or doesn't hold. I can be free to enjoy, bask in and relish my life as it is, with all its ups and downs, challenges, and triumphs, without wishing it otherwise.

It showed me that there is always more freedom to be found, always more wonder, always more peace, and joy. Those things are what we are made of, and they are found here, now, in this moment. I will be forever grateful for those who pointed me in this direction, and those who continue to point, even when mankind seems determined to look the other way. For a girl who thought she was doomed to the grey, second-rate version, it's a beautiful thing, this life in glorious technicolour.

Adapted from an article published in Magnificent Metamorphosis Magazine, Issue 2, June 2020

Chapter 20 – Leanne Taylor

"When they go low, we go high" – Michelle Obama

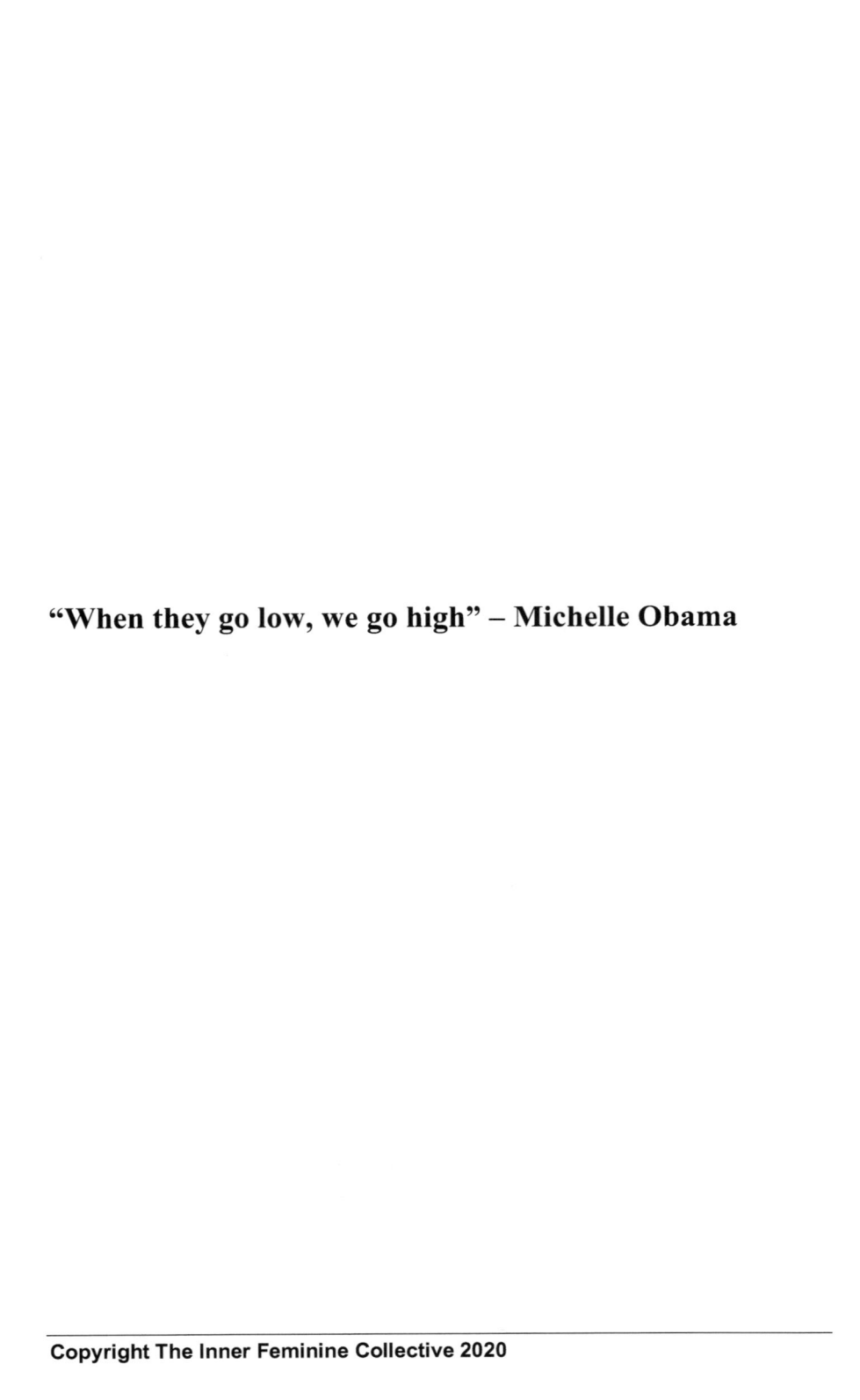

Looking in the mirror, I did not recognise myself. Who was I? When was the last time I did something for me? Practiced the self-care and love I now promote so much? Is this really the life I chose? Why do I feel like there is more? Why do I feel trapped, knowing I have choices, when so many others do not?

We are told so often that greed is not an attractive trait. So, saying out loud that I wanted more felt horribly wrong. Guilt overwhelmed me for even daring think I could have more. Once the guilt roared like a lion, but now, although it still lingers, it is quieter, even mouse-like! But back then, it roared.

Imagine this. Married to a doctor, with two children. A great job, big house, holidays. Wanting for nothing. I had created a beautiful life, one that I thought I wanted! One influenced by the goals and wants of others I knew, created in the image of a definition of successful that I saw on social media, and everywhere around me. Adopting those values as my own. Conditioned by society, and my upbringing, to believe that this was what I wanted.

I should have been happy to live this life, to have all those things. And I was grateful for everything. But deep inside I still had a gut-wrenching desire for something more. Something that I could not even articulate, because I did not really know what "more" was.

Well I did just that, I said "I want more!"

I feel no shame, because now I know that what I was seeking was a life of purpose. To feel passionate about helping change the world and showing my daughters that there was so much more out there. It was as if I had suddenly been called to take action. To step up and do more, to get more!

Then came the incident as I like to call it. The sign to make the change, to leave that life I was living. This story is not about that so I will allow you, the reader, to interpret what this sign was however you wish to.

Just like that I became a statistic. Another broken family. Someone flipped a switch and I instantly felt a weight lifted from my shoulders. My decisions were my own. Amazingly I did not fail! I learned as I went, and I grew. My wings were no longer clipped.

I had not realised how much I was changing my life for someone else. Without them taking my feelings and dreams into consideration. I had to learn to find myself again, discover who I was, what in life I wanted.

My best friend was my biggest supporter. You would never have guessed he suffered from depression. Always the life and soul of the party, always smiling. He always gave good positive advice when needed.

Losing him broke me, but also spurred me to follow my calling. Details are not necessary here, but when the police told me they had found him I will never forget the noise that left my lungs. I felt physical pain from saying goodbye to him.

I spiralled downwards, forgetting things, drinking more often than I should, not wanting to get out of bed, eating less. And again, guilt crept in. I felt guilty about feeling any happiness with him gone.

Then, on a walk, I saw a white feather drop in front of me. Later that evening I had a dream. To this day, I still cannot describe the dream, but it was peaceful and calm. A welcome break, after months of nightmares and insomnia. Up until now, I would have told you all things spiritual were rubbish and that anything that could not be explained by science simply could not be true.

Next morning, I woke up feeling…not better exactly, but with a new perspective. I knew that I had to help change the narrative for people with mental health.

I started running, and found exercise was great therapy. It was my "me" time. An hour of music to heal the soul, played at full blast while I moved my body, working to make it stronger. My body and mind grew stronger together.

I cleared my social media and unfollowed everyone whose feed did not fill me with joy, made me feel less, or fed my guilt. I made a point to post the good, the bad, and the downright ugly. There were definitely a few of those moments!

With this new passion and purpose came a new mind-set. They say vision is everything and I had that. Amazingly, people with similar passions reached out to me. Some have become friends. My newfound confidence enabled me to step beyond my imposter syndrome and I launched a not for profit to help increase awareness of the link between movement and the mind. How exercise can be used as a form of therapy for those with mental health issues. But also, for everyone who wants to look after their mental health and protect it against the stresses and strains of modern life.

I have grown my knowledge and embraced other therapies and ways to move energy. Meditation and cold showers (you must build up to a full 30 seconds!) are now part of my daily life and routine.

Allowing yourself to believe and leaning into your power allows a new energy to enter. There is no doubt that the saying "The Universe has your back" is true! I have proved it.

The message I wanted to convey is out there, and has been embraced by many. With such positivity there is only room to grow. I am still learning; to lean into my power, to trust my instincts, to refuse to give in to my imposter syndrome, and to believe in myself fully. I teach what I know, and I know that that there is fulfilment to be had in life. You do not have to "settle" for anything.

In the words of Little Mix; "These wings were made to fly."

Chapter 21 – Mariella O'Brien

"We spend so much time trying to 'earn' and 'justify' our place here on Earth. We do not have to earn our place here. We can't. We are here by grace, and our very existence is a gift. And the only thing that's up to us is how we use that gift."
Michael Neill

The Good Girl

I was born and raised in Bulgaria surrounded by a large loving family. Growing up I was the good girl. Shy and sensitive, tuned in to other people's feelings, I tried to be who, and do what everybody expected of me and please everyone around me. I loved making my family proud and happy.

I come from a family of highly educated and respected, driven individuals who believed that education and hard work pave the way to success in life. My parents and grandparents invested time and money in my education. Described by one of my teachers as determined and painfully ambitious, I was programmed to believe that I could achieve anything. As long as I applied myself and worked hard. Many opportunities were lovingly provided for me along with the underlying expectation for excellence. Or at least this is how the quiet sensitive girl perceived them at the time. Inevitably, aiming so high led to an occasional disappointment. The thought "I am not good enough" was seeded in my subconscious at an early age.

One of my earliest memories was going with Granny to meet the piano teacher that my cousin was taking lessons with. The teacher played a note on the piano and asked me to sing along. I was too shy to even make a sound. I don't remember if I sang at all, but the teacher quickly concluded that 'She does not have an ear for music'. I never got to have piano lessons; I wasn't good enough.

Another memory that sticks in my mind is my experience with gymnastics. I had the "special" privilege of being granted a place in a well-known gymnastics academy, because my dad worked in the army at the time.

Rhythmic gymnastics was big in Bulgaria in the 80s. The Bulgarian team were winning gold at World and European championships. I still have no idea why my parents thought it was a good idea for ME to do gymnastics! It was torture and humiliating. I was taller and heavier built than most of the girls at the academy. I remember one of the coaches telling me I had to eat less if I ever wanted to be any good at gymnastics. I refused to go back after that. This experience planted another seed in my brain. A whole load of weight and body issues that persisted throughout my teenage years and strengthening the existing idea; I wasn't good enough.

I excelled in my school life. In primary school I achieved top marks. I volunteered for every position of responsibility – from head girl to school representative at the Youth Council, which was part of the City Council. "A proper little communist activist", as my husband now jokingly remarks. From the age of 9 I had to prepare reports and speak in front of large school assemblies. This never came easily to me, and often my lips would break out in strings of cold sores after speaking. There were also perks from holding those positions. I went on an exchange trip to Moscow and Kiev with the Youth Council. We spent time volunteering for the Red Cross.

I was making my family proud. With their encouragement, I set my sights on a prestigious foreign language high school with competitive entry exams. I studied hard, put in many hours and had extra private tuition. I enjoyed the studying but when it came to the exam, I did not do so well, I didn't make the grade. Maybe the high expectations got to me.

I worked really hard. But once again; I wasn't good enough.

I don't have many good memories from my high school days. I enjoyed my own company and spent endless hours reading in the 'safety' of my own room. I preferred the world in my head to the outside world.

I craved connection and friendship but found it difficult to reach out. I tried hard to fit in and was befriended by the popular girls in class. Later, I realised that I was their secret weapon when it came to maths tests and homework assignments. However, in the latter part of my high school years, I did make two very loyal friends who have been a big part of my adult life.

Another memory, but a lovely one. We had just moved to a new apartment. I was in my room and I heard my name being called from outside. Two girls from my building had found out my name and were curious to meet me. I was excited that someone was reaching out and wanted to be friends, but I was too nervous and shy to just open the window and say "Hi!"

I was lurking by my window with the lights turned off. After a while they shouted; "We know you're there, we can see your shadow!" I was embarrassed, but I was also grateful. Glad that they did not give up on me. I ended up going out to meet them that evening. They helped me come out of my shell, and they became trusted friends, with whom I shared many adventures, in my teenage years and into adulthood. This was my first experience of the collective power of women supporting other women and raising each other up.

My search for external approval and validation continued. At university I studied International Business and Politics to a master's degree level. On completing that I went to work for the Bulgarian Government, working in the Foreign Relations Department of the Secretary for Transport. At age 22 I found myself travelling around Europe on diplomatic missions, writing ministers' speeches and interpreting; Bulgarian-English, for government officials. Attending UN conferences and even leading negotiations on international transport corridors. I was soon heading up a team of civil servants and set for a high-flying career.

Yet again my family was proud. I was successful. But by who's definition? It is true I enjoyed the thrill of those experiences and adventures. But my role brought extreme stress and high pressure. A lot of responsibility for such young shoulders to carry.

Secretly I was longing for different adventures, further afield. I dreamt of learning to scuba-dive and being a marine biologist working to protect coral reefs. My interest in the underwater world did not lead to a career but I did meet my husband, who was writing for Diver magazine in the UK. After a brief long-distance relationship, I left my "high-flying" career and my family behind. I moved to the UK to start a new chapter of my life.

This was a big bold jump into the unknown for me. But I was ready to spread my wings. It was probably the first time that I had stood up for myself, trusted my intuition, and followed what felt like the right path for me. It is amazing how life unfolds when we listen to those inner callings and let them guide us. It would be a long time before I recognised that though!

Moving to a new country was tough. Everything was new and unfamiliar. I left the support network of family and friends behind. My previous career status and credentials from Bulgaria counted for nothing in the UK. Bulgaria was not yet a member of the EU, and my qualifications and university degrees were not recognised. Even my driving license was invalid. My confidence was at an all-time-low.

My husband and I decided that to help my transition, I should go back to university and get another master's degree. I had always dreamt of studying in the UK. With hindsight, I can see that I chose the safe path. I knew how to be a good student. I loved losing myself in the library, and I knew it would please my parents.

Studying for a master's degree was not a walk in the park. But I dug deep and worked hard. I enjoyed it too. I was proud when I was granted my Master of Science degree in International Business Management, now it was time for me to face the real world and find a job.

This was the hardest part. Many job applications were submitted. Numerous interviews and assessment centres attended. The process was relentless, and rejections were coming back from every direction. I was applying for graduate training schemes in large corporates. My quiet sensitive nature was not a good fit for those selection events. I had great ideas but struggled to get them heard. I was having no success finding a job, and I started to feel depressed. I had to find a good job to prove myself once more.

At that point in my life I had no idea that external recognition, job title and size of pay cheque do not equate to success and happiness. It would take another decade for that penny to drop!

Things took a turn for the better when I started to volunteer in a charity shop in my local town. This gave me something to get out of bed for. I loved my time there. I was making a difference and being of service - my confidence was buoyed up. I got a sense that giving is worth more than receiving.

Soon after that, I was offered a temporary admin job at Barclays Bank. This was the start of a 11-year career. With determination and grit, I worked my way around the organisation and moved up the corporate career ladder. I was feeling ambitious and prepared to be out of my comfort zone, just so I could tick the boxes that would lead to the next promotion. I was determined to be "successful" once more.

Every rung I climbed on the career ladder brought more pressure to fit into the extrovert-male-dominated idea of success. My quiet nature felt like a weakness, something I had to overcome if I really wanted to be successful. The "not visible enough" and "not assertive enough" appraisals confirmed my gut feeling. The "needs to speak up more in meetings" feedback; the giant open plan offices; the endless days spent on conference calls, competing for airtime.
This was a time when I was expected to work to strengthen my weaknesses and improve in areas where I was deemed not good enough. Focused on the negative, instead of playing to my strengths. Another decade of trying to fit into a box, searching for external validation and proof of my worth.

Even after my children were born, I kept going. Allowing my career status to define me. Chasing success as defined by society. I had the big job title and huge responsibilities. Long working hours and I was miserable and exhausted. I never felt good enough and I was suffering physically and mentally. In all this pushing and striving, I lost "me". I could see no meaning in any of it.

The shift from ambition to meaning

I remember sitting in my garden thinking "There must be more to life than this!" It was time to step off the ever-spinning hamster wheel of the corporate world. It was the only possible decision. Time to jump into the unknown again. It felt liberating!

It took me months to unwind, I was a tightly coiled spring. I began considering new ways to be in the world, I spent time on learning and working on self-development. Oh boy, it was so hard to admit and accept that self-care had to become my priority if I was to come back to myself and make sense of what I needed to do next.

I invested in my personal growth and hired a coach, I spent months reading and searching for answers. Self-reflection and writing brought clarity and meaning.

The first part of my journey was to understand and accept my introverted nature. With this came the realisation that who I am IS good enough! I finally worked out that the desire to be perfect is toxic and I gradually learned to take imperfect action – setting up a private community for introverts, learning various modalities of coaching, jetting off to coaching intensives abroad.

I re-wrote my definition of success and started forging my life on my own terms. I was in search of purpose for my life. I knew I wanted to be a force for good in the world, no matter how small my contribution. To be of service to others. To make the world a better place. I just had not figured out how yet.

This played perfectly into the hands of the self-help industry, which is readily available to try and fix you and give you the answers. I threw myself into it fully, consuming other people's wisdom instead of looking inside for my own answers. I began to believe that I needed fixing. That I needed other people's input to help me run my house and parent my children, find my purpose and live a fulfilling life.

Then I came across the inside-out understanding of how life works.

What a relief to know that I am not broken, and I was never damaged, that I am fundamentally OK, and I have everything I need inside of me; I am enough!

A glimpse into our true nature

This beautiful understanding finally put all the pieces of the puzzle together for me. Initially, I got it on an intellectual level. But as I explored and played with it further, the insights came rolling in. I would be gifted weeks of blissful existence floating in wellbeing and peace, but then I would get lost in my thoughts and feelings again, and start striving to fix my experience. Trying to push certain emotions away or judging myself for feeling down when I should know better. I saw how it played out in certain areas of my life but not in others. I uncovered many blind spots over a few years. All part of the exploration of how life really works.

I felt moved to share what I had learned to help empower others and started building my own coaching practice once more. I knew I wanted to share this understanding with young people, so they can have an easier journey through life. Knowing they are always supported by their true nature, the wisdom of life. That we all are.

I love working with young people and seeing the pure potential they are. I want to nurture and support them, so they can be free from the limitations of their mind and their life circumstances. To help them get in touch with their innate wellbeing and unbreakable nature. Empower them to set themselves up for success and happiness on their own terms. The kind of input I could have benefitted from when I was younger.

A powerful and worthwhile cause. Yet for almost two years I have hidden behind other people's projects, found excuses, and waited for the right moment. I have had this burning mission inside me, but not found a way to put it out into the world.

I have read every single 3P book and blogpost in existence, attended numerous practitioner trainings. Been the constant presence at home for my children and husband. The mum who volunteers for every school fair and class trip. The woman that gives her time freely to any other worthwhile cause but not her own burning mission and desire.

Why I hear you ask? Why after several years of self-discovery, the shedding of limiting beliefs, and extensive spiritual exploration am I still stuck in the shadows? I guess it is all part of the game of life – the exploration never ends.

I was the good girl, the A grade student, the career woman who worked so hard to please and prove her worth. Who got put down so many times while trying to fit in that she developed a very harsh inner critic. The good girl who was so afraid to fail, she had to have it all worked out before she even started. Because being visible and making mistakes, whilst standing up for what you believe is scary. It leaves you feeling vulnerable.

All of this was playing out subconscious. Until I chose to notice and shine a light on it.

Because life is not a straight line, it's a spiral. You continually circle back to the lessons you thought you had already learned, in order to see deeper truths.

Because we can never see the whole map for our exciting adventures. The path reveals itself one step at a time. And it is a matter of trust, trust in the wisdom we are made of, the same wisdom that is with us every moment. Providing fresh guidance every step of the way. But not before we have taken the all important first step and committed to the journey.

What is behind that vulnerability and fear of failing? I know now that it is only a reaction to an imagined version of the future, made up by our wonderfully creative thinking. And what is fear protecting? It is only protecting an idea of who we are or should be.

Our self-identity, the collection of thoughts and beliefs we acquire along the way is composed of thought. Our mind stores it all away and uses it to protect us, to keep us safe. It is the same identity that says, "Go on, get out there, be more visible" and then criticises and says "You just made a fool of yourself!"

And so on, and so forth. But we are more than that!

We are SO much more than a collection of thoughts and beliefs, our self-identity. We are all a oneness, an intelligence that makes planets and holds universes together.

We are not the stories we create in our minds. We do not have to believe those stories or act them out. We are the storyteller. The space where stories and experiences arise.

As I see this for myself more deeply, I can now engage more fully with life. I can show up as myself, authentic and vulnerable. I speak my mission into the world, to allow it to come to existence. I can be gentle and compassionate with myself and others for our humanness. I can see the struggles as gifts that point us back to freedom.

Can you step out of your story today and catch a glimpse of the space between the lines - your true nature?

You are enough, you have always been enough! Follow your inner calling and let life express through you. You are here for a reason!

Chapter 22 - Wendi May New

Copyright The Inner Feminine Collective 2020

"Spread your wings and fly! Go anywhere you want!"
Wendi May New

I am tired out, sitting on a train with my daughter, returning home from an all-expenses paid trip to London. I am wondering if this is the start of a new journey and where it will lead me. During our 2-day trip we have stayed in a hotel and had a wonderful meal in a great restaurant who want to display my artwork! I want to pinch myself. Could this be real?

And then I remember other nights. Where I sat by a window, looking out over a railway track at different houses and trying to imagine where my daughter and I would end up. How did these changes in my life come about? Let me tell you about my journey.

I am 52. I was born in North Yorkshire. In my twenties spent some time living and working in Holland, moving back to the UK in 1996.

My career has been varied and interesting, mainly because my career choices have often come about because of me being in the right place at the right time!

I have always loved arts and crafts and studied for an HND in Art and Design at Sunderland University. My passion for art has been the thread running throughout my working life.

At various times I have studied for other qualifications, including a Certificate of Education and Training, and a Graphic Arts Degree.

When I returned to the UK, I took a job working as an admin assistant in the NHS for a while, before moving to a Mental Health resource centre, recruited as a technical instructor in screen printing.

I expanded into engraving, did some business admin, and eventually became the NVQ co-ordinator.

Between 1999 and 2006 I worked in Further Education in Cambridge, utilising my Cert Ed and becoming a middle manager in Art and Design.

From there, I went to work in a prison for a while, using my Arts qualifications. I wrote a course in Art, Design and Animation for the inmates. A group of my students went on to win an award for an animated film they had created!

I had an interesting and enjoyable life, doing things that I loved.

I met my daughter Hollie's Dad in 2000. We relocated to Lowestoft in Suffolk. Hollie was born in 2007, but my relationship with my partner had broken down and it became so toxic that we split up 7 months later.

For just over a year I tried to carry on, with continued abuse from my partner, trying to cope with the mortgage on my own, while taking care of Hollie and keeping my job. But eventually, on the verge of being made homeless, I had to admit defeat. You can't make choices when you are homeless.

So I gave up my job and moved 260 miles north to move back in with Mum, taking over her spare room with 10 plastic boxes of belongings, 2 cats and my daughter. I could not quite believe what had happened to my life.

The breakup had knocked me for six. I felt erased, rubbed out, a nobody, that I was not a person anymore. I could not quite believe what I had become.

I looked down at the floor when I walked past anyone. I did not want to talk or let them see my face. I had nothing to say. I was an empty shell.

While at my mums I talked to a lady who pointed out that I had experienced domestic abuse.

About six weeks later I was offered a place in a woman's refuge. Which was where I found myself sitting gazing out of that window wondering what was next.

The refuge was a safe place. Somewhere where I could find some headspace, uncurl and start thinking about beginning again. About building the kind of life I wanted for Hollie.

The staff were lovely and very supportive. Encouraging all the residents to help themselves, providing structure to our days, keeping us busy.

I received lots of help and advice in the refuge, and I was advised to file for bankruptcy to sort the debt out. I was struggling with dealing with that, as well as all the emotional fall out from my situation. But I had a dedicated support worker, and the refuge was close to both my Mum and my Dad.

I joined a gym and began taking better care of myself. Then the staff recommended that I join something called The Freedom Project.

Run every Saturday over several weeks the program was designed to help women like me deal with the abuse we had experienced. I did not have high hopes for it, in fact I was very cynical about whether it was for me. But I went anyway.

The project challenged us to look back at our experiences and frame differently. To face events from our past and deal with them. It was a turning point for me. Something I believe every woman in my situation should have access to.

It brought tears, fears, and realisation. That I could learn to make better choices. It brought me back, slowly. A small part of me started to see some hope. My mum said that she could see me rising like a phoenix out of the ashes. She said she wanted to see me smile again and said how I had always been a happy fun girl and she missed me. Now I had a chance to get that person back. I was on the road to recovery. And then, after six months I was offered a house. Hollie and I had a new home!

While I was in the refuge one of my friend's husbands had asked me if I would be interested in a paid artwork job for the local prison. I found out a bit more about it and decided it was something I could do. I had a purpose again. I sat and did the drawings on a little table in the refuge, in the evenings and, when Hollie was at nursery.

My cousin helped me out, scanning my designs so that I could get them printed onto huge aluminium sheets. They would be delivered to him so that I could see them before they were sent to the prison to be installed, as I could not go into the prison to see them in place.

Because I had been made bankrupt, I had no bank account, so the money was paid into my Dad's account and he helped me to buy a car, a laptop, a fridge a washing machine and some other bits for our new home. The rest was put aside for paying for the murals to be printed.

Dad said, "You could probably make a living doing this." He always encouraged me.

I had also been volunteering at the nursery group we attended while we were at the refuge, helping the children have fun with arts and crafts. The Sure Start centre saw my drawings and asked me to do some paid sessions for them as an "artist."

That went well and then they asked me to create a mural for their new extended nursery. It was a beautiful project to be part of, and when Rosemary Shrager came along to open the centre I was very proud.

Then the primary school attached to the centre asked if I could do some murals for them! Work was coming in, I loved working with the staff and the children, and I had money in the bank!

I registered as self-employed in 2010. I was asked to be a school governor, and I started running art clubs in schools. I had won awards for some of my work. Hollie and I were settled in our home. My business was growing. Our lives had turned around.

Fast forward to 2020. The recent lockdown due to COVID-19 brought a lot of challenges. My workshops dried up and I had to get to grips with online workshops using Zoom. But I also attended zoom sessions in pastels, portrait painting and charcoal! Improving my skills. I have had to learn to market myself differently.

I also managed to stay in touch with my running buddies, fellow volunteers at Park Run, and artists in the co-operative I am a member of.

Home-schooling definitely created issues for Hollie and I along with some social anxiety.

Copyright The Inner Feminine Collective 2020

But we have come through it! The gallery has re-opened and paintings are starting to sell. Art classes have started to resume. And I am starting to rebrand myself.
And then came the invitation from the restaurant in London! Flipping amazing!

I could not quite believe it. They want ME as an ARTIST!. Stars and Royalty eat there! They want signage, canvases, illustrations! Artwork on the walls! My art on their menus, hats, merchandise! They want wine and olive oil labels!
I did suggest that they could offer it to another artist, even offered to recommend a few. But they replied "We want you! We want your art on our walls!"

Can you tell how excited I am?

We had a WONDERFUL trip to London!

I am here to tell you that no matter what happens, no matter how bad things get, you can always turn your life around. People used to say to me "It will all be ok."

And I thought, what do you know about it? But they were right!

I have a roof over my head; food on the table; no one is telling me what to do.

I feel like I know myself a lot better now.

And I feel I can offer some words of wisdom to anyone who is struggling:
- Be open to opportunity
- Don't give up hope
- Don't be afraid to ask for help

- Take each day as it comes
- Be patient and take each day as it comes
- Who says you can't?

When I left the refuge one of the ladies said to me "Spread your wings and fly! Go anywhere you want!"

And I am!

Chapter 23 - Sara Calgie

"I always thought that I was my mind
And this body too
Until I asked myself what is looking
Looking through"
Nick Mulvey

My Education

My early teen years were a struggle. Some difficult experiences led to me not attending secondary school regularly in my early teen years. I absconded, a lot!

Times were different then. It was not considered to be the school's responsibility to support the emotional wellbeing of the child. I managed to slip off the radar and found myself in a very vulnerable position. The support offered to me at the time was from people who were also on the fringes of society. A mixed bunch of people. Vulnerable themselves, with mental health problems, and some of them engaging in criminal activities.

I consider myself lucky to have negotiated that phase of my life relatively unscathed. Despite their issues, these people were present and kind. They saw me and held space for me.

Later I attempted to re-sit my GCSE exams. But I fell into the same patterns of behaviour as before. I wasn't bad or thick, but I was not able to manage my emotions. Particularly when I felt afraid. I learned to avoid situations where I felt uncomfortable.

I had no coping strategies, no support network. I was experiencing serious trauma and blamed myself for not being able to do the things I needed to do, that I felt the world expected me to do. I hated myself.

Then I went to art college. I found a space where I could participate, communicate, and express myself in a different way. Engaging with people in a way I had not before. It was something I could do easily.

Something I cared about. I took every opportunity to make choices and be creative. I was in control, and I found my voice. I thrived. It was like learning a new language. One that I was fluent in. It was exhilarating. I was contributing, learning, growing, and developing. My confidence soared. I made friends and I felt that I was fitting in. I went further and progressed to another further art college.

After that I started work in design. I had done well at college and found a sponsor from a luxury handmade shoemaker in Pall Mall. He sponsored my final collection in Men's footwear, and I began to climb the ladder in that industry. I had gained experience in design studios, designing, pattern cutting and making samples in the heart of design offices.

With my newfound confidence I excelled in my employment. But even though I was doing well, the belief that I was not good enough resurfaced. It was rooted deep inside me and lingered.

I believed that I lacked something because I had not been able to access the kind of education I believed my peers held in high esteem. That somehow, I had cheated my way into a 'normal life.' So, I limited myself.

I swapped the design room for retail, quickly becoming manager of a lovely designer clothes shop in Covent Garden. Earning twice as much as a shoe designer at the start of their career! Having always supported myself financially, I grabbed the opportunity to earn. I was ambitious and talented, winning 'Salesperson of the year' soon after.

I grew up in the city of Durham. A university town. I attended a lovely, small primary school in the city centre after my parents divorced, when I was eight.

The children I went to school with were from very diverse backgrounds. Most of them had parents who worked as academics at the university. My class was multicultural. The adults around me were both interesting and interested. As my own parents had separated, I began to spend time with other families.

My best friend's dad was a physics lecturer. Durham University's new £2.5 million Microscopy facility is now named after him.

In this atmosphere, I grew up believing that academic accomplishment was something to aspire to. Amongst my friend's parents there was a Greek Orthodox priest, a painter, a furniture maker, chemistry professors and a bistro owner! They had full and vibrant lives and were creative. They had meaningful discussions about causes; Lebanon, Gadaffi, CND or 'Save the Whale.' They were passionate and social in their bohemian 70's homes.

I was excited by them all, weaving between their homes for dinner. Before and after swimming, gymnastics, ice skating or ballet. With Enid Blyton style roams round the observatory hill, the riverbank, and the palace green outside the Cathedral.

Home was very different. My mum was juggling jobs. There was never time or enough money to be sociable. She worked long days as a nanny, cleaner and youth leader. All at once, just to keep a roof over our heads. Being a single parent in the late 70s and early 80s was unusual. Back then there were only two children at my school from what was called a "broken home".

We spent weekends with my grandparents in Newcastle. Granddad worked night shifts in the shipyards, returning at the crack of dawn. Grandma would take me into town to look at the shops, so that he could sleep in peace. I spent a lot of time with her during school holidays, while Mum was at work. My brother and I were expected to behave at all times.

I loved the university environment. I spent hours at the home of Mrs Kenworthy, the Dean of St Mary's College, whilst my Mum worked to make her home sparkle. It was full of curiosities from her time living in Africa, including stuffed animals which she told me all about.

Mum's nanny job, for Dr Sweet and his wife, included me too. We all walked home from school and spent time together, until they returned from work. We would leave just as the family sat down to dinner.

Mum's third workplace, 'Youthie' was a different way of life. Set in a small colliery village a couple of miles out of Durham City, in the countryside. During the miners' strike I noticed the club getting bigger and bigger.
The social deprivation was very evident, and I saw it up close.

I went into one house where the stairs had been chopped down and replaced with a rope ladder. The wood was needed for warmth. I stood in queues to collect tins of European surplus tinned meat. It did not bother me. We were in receipt of "dinner tickets" and that meant we had to queue separately for our school dinner.

Despite living with very little, at home our culture was strong. There may only have been a slice of toast for breakfast. But mum would still set the table beautifully, and there would be a vase of wildflowers. She was amazing at making the most out of whatever was available. I will always be sad that when I started to feel that I was not good enough I projected that onto Mum.

We did not invite people to our house, there was never any extra to share. I was a sociable child living with my Mam and my brother, who were quite introverted and self-contained characters. I felt stifled. I was spirited and outgoing, craving stimulation.

The family life I glimpsed in the homes of my peers enticed me away from my own home. I spent all the time I could wherever I was welcome and started to sleep over at other people's houses, becoming increasingly independent.

Holidays were taken with other families who had interesting friends, made music, ate interesting food, and had well-meaning parents who got a kick out of bringing me into their homes. Soothing their socially conscious egos because I came from a broken home. They had heard about the difficulties my Dad was having, and how it was affecting my Mum, even though they were no longer together.

I ticked a box like volunteering or attending a 'faith supper.' The point is - I always valued education. I understood its currency, not just for the academic achievement, but for the discipline, compliance, and conformity it confers. It says, "Here is a group of people who can communicate their ideas, they will be useful." I wanted to be like that. I wanted to have an interesting life. Be ambitious. Be accepted and accepting of everything offered to me.

After primary school, I moved to a different comprehensive school than my friends. I had moved catchment area when my parents split. I waited two years to join them at the same school. It was hard to lose touch, and when I did get a place, they had moved into new classes and friendship groups. I felt displaced. But I was good at finding people to join in with.

I started a job in a lovely bistro bar, working in the kitchen at 13. I felt so grown up. I floated around a bit, fitting in wherever I could.

One day I ended up with some new friends at a party. They were older than me, and I was too grown up for my age. I don't even know why I went, or what I was looking for. It was raided by the police. They stopped it and sent everyone home.

We scattered and I left with a few boys from my school who were a little older. A local man we had never met invited us to come and sit in his shed until everything settled down. It felt quite exhilarating, a little naughty even. I hadn't even had a boyfriend at that age and was completely unaware of the vulnerable position I'd put myself in.

In a moment, it all turned bad as the man changed. He locked us all in, putting a big padlock on the door, before turning his attention to me, raping me in front of those terrified kids. For hours we were locked in together in this surreal experience. I never spoke to them about it, and even went to work and then school in the couple of days afterwards. When I did tell my friend at school at lunchtime, she went to the telephone box to ring and tell her mum.

Next thing I knew, I was taken away in a panda car by the police. In full view of all the pupils of that 1970's comprehensive school, with big glazed metal windows overlooking the reception and courtyard. It felt like every schoolchild watched me escorted out that day. The following week I was dropped off again at school to resume my normal life. But that was never going to happen.

Years later, I remember reading Maya Angelou's story. After being raped, she told too. Her attacker was found and attacked, dying as a result of his injuries. She felt that she had killed a man and stopped talking. As if her words were the weapon that killed him. It resonated. I had an acute wish that my attack would cause no further harm.

Released after serving five years in prison, my rapist took his own life. I remember feeling responsible. I read more about Maya.

"If you get give, if you teach learn."

This stayed with me, as I put myself back together. Going back to school was so difficult. I tried but it was so hard. It was easier to go, leave and roam about for the days, years that followed. I managed to get one GCSE in art because they took coursework and I drew. I drew and drew and drew!!

I am a hard worker. But there is a limit to what can be achieved with hard work alone, especially in fields like education. Education develops through research and evidence-based practice – it is rooted in academia. I came to education by accident. It was not until my early 30s that I was ready to be educated.

By chance, an unscheduled day off led to me offering to help in my young son's school. By the end of that day, I knew that I wanted to change my career. I was ready to leave the creative sector. Having worked in fashion and footwear design, I had crossed over into interiors. Then I ran my own company. I was very proud. It had been incredibly conceptual and innovative, at that time. But it all felt shallow and pretentious in the end.

Motherhood changed me. I had become more socially conscious. That unexpected experience in school showed me how wonderful the school culture could be, and I was inspired.

But what I really wanted to do was nurture, not teach. To do something in alignment with my soul's purpose. I was going to have to learn, to start again.

An access class, and a year of volunteer work later, I was accepted to study for BA in Education for the foundation year at Durham University. It took me three months to fill in the application form, and the day I matriculated was one of the proudest days of my life. A new beginning. This time I was the driver. I was captain of my ship.

I had struggled to overcome those long-held feelings of disadvantage. Here I was, an experienced and capable mother of two, who had excelled at work despite a "lack of education". After years of feeling like a rejected child, of being a token inclusion in other people's lives, a wildcard. "Dippy Sara". Feeling inferior to next to my high achieving teenage friends, with the confidence that comes from a life of privilege. They had been high achievers all their lives. They were not scared to fail!

Of course, none of these things was true. They were students from diverse backgrounds who all had their own stories. But these were the stories I invented, stories I told myself.

That I was disadvantaged. That it was obvious to everyone else, that they were being kind and generous, but would inevitably see that I was no good.

This was the narrative that ran through my core. All made up in my head.

I studied development and learning. I learned about the thalamus which is part of the limbic system. It is the hub the brain uses to select data. I became aware that I sometimes brought unconscious bias into my decision making.

I learned to prime my brain about what to be alert to. The 'unconscious noticing' and association from memories, had the potential to affect what my brain assigned. Logical and emotional thoughts were muddled and disorganised. Time and time again my brain steered me down a path I did not choose. It would have been so easy to avoid risk and give up.

Limiting subconscious beliefs had shaped my life so far. Now I was onto it! I learned how our brains have a tendency to being risk averse. I had to fight a battle with myself to overcome this. I was lucky - I had over a decade of creativity to fall back on. Creativity had given me habits, skills and qualities that enabled me to work towards visions. I explored and discovered, following my own interests and intuition.

Working in the arts, I had learned to be curious, disciplined, and persistent. To communicate and use imagination to create original ideas. These skills now supported my learning. I conquered my lack mindset. The creative skills I had allowed me to turn off autopilot and be proactive rather than passive in my learning.

Developing creativity and creative skill is a series of small failures. The challenge and difficulty that you overcome when you are learning is innately rewarding, increases confidence and leads to more learning opportunities.

In my foundation year I did an overview of A level sciences. I realised that if you stand for science that you stand for change. I reframed failure, realising that failed attempts could still teach. That discovery comes through experimentation, rebranding "can't" as "can't do yet".

I realised that I had a wild imagination, highly visual, and this served me well. Helped me focus on what I wanted, propelled me towards my vision of the future, if I just brought sufficient action. Visual literacy became the subject of my dissertation and set me on a path. As I learned more about the history of school curriculum, I let myself off the hook. I dropped any blame I had directed to myself in the past. And to any staff for not 'seeing me.' It just wasn't their job.

As I said earlier, when I was in school, staff were not responsible for the social, emotional, or physical well-being of the pupils. It was not that they did not care but it was not in their remit to act in a supporting role. It is now! Times have changed.

As a classroom teacher myself, I saw how the difficulties of students could be eased by reframing the subject in a more personal, relevant, and meaningful way. It is a hard aspiration, because the education system is set up to measure by assessment and productivity. We are required to track each pupil's personal progress.

I work in an area where around 40% of children live in poverty. Many are experiencing deprivation, and I know that is affecting their ability to learn. Many have lack mindset, unconscious negativity, limited experience, and low aspirations. I know that if I can engage with these children and reach them through more creative learning experiences, then I can build their confidence and communication.

I can use visual art, and through engagement, I can teach them about other things in the curriculum. The arts are a great leveller and apart from teaching it for its own sake, we can use it as a conduit to other areas of learning.

I am now an arts educator. After working as a primary teacher, I founded a community art studio. The aim is to support creativity, visual art habits and skills and raise the perceived value of arts in education. As well as working with schools and families, we target our work to support children who are experiencing disadvantage, using our surplus to offer funded arts continued professional development to primary teachers.

Many children who have experienced trauma will use self-limiting beliefs for the rest of their lives, to protect themselves. We hope to develop their vision through supporting them to access learning in a different way, as art helps children become more like themselves.

It has taken me half of my life to truly know that sometimes it is the bad experiences that prepare you for your purpose. If you can learn then you can teach, support others and be of service. My creative mind helped me manage my present, visualise my future and help other people create not only art, but create themselves.

Chapter 24 - Simone Lanham

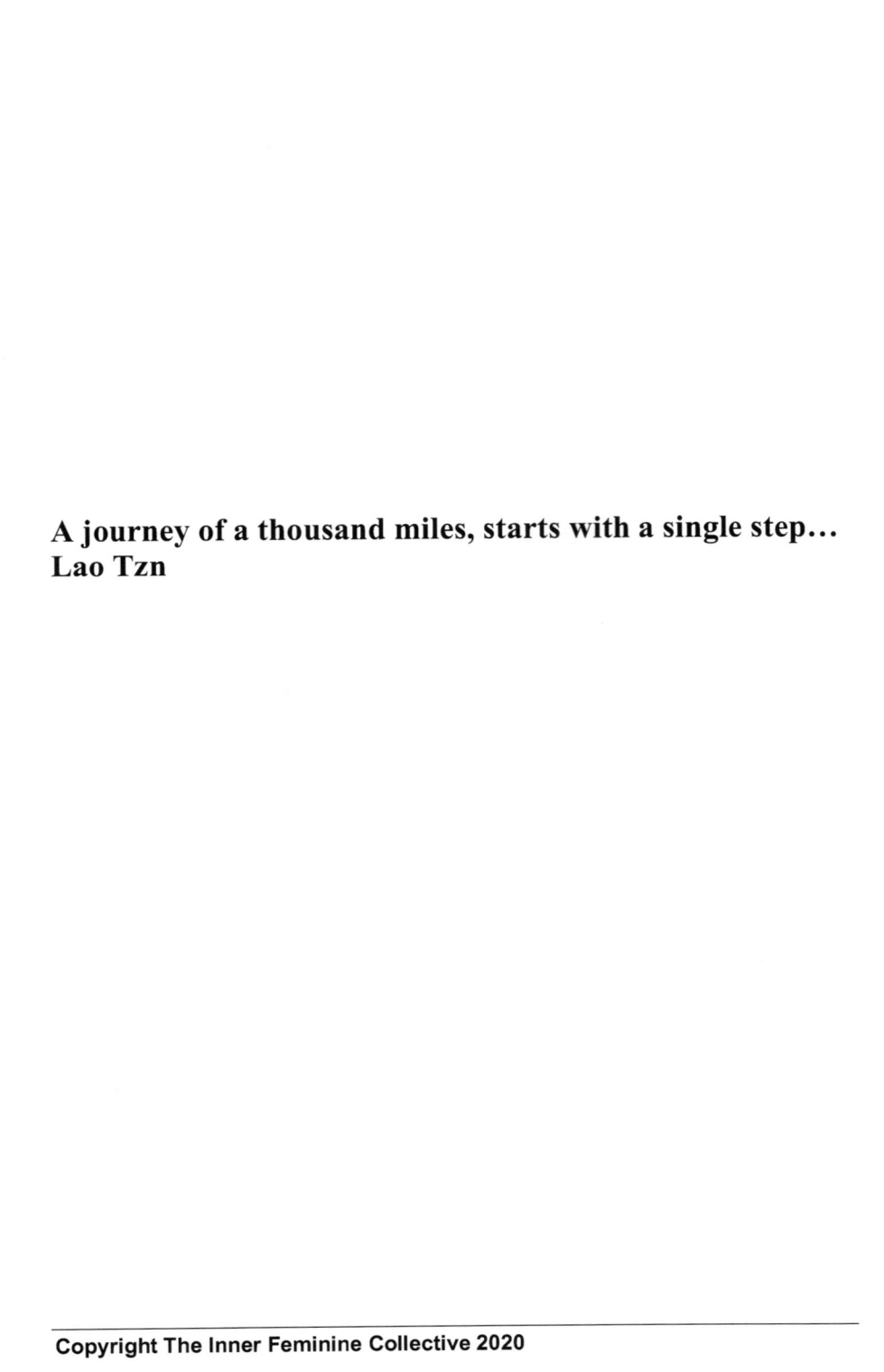

**A journey of a thousand miles, starts with a single step…
Lao Tzn**

The journey to be seen and heard

My story is about finding my truth and purpose through overcoming adversity.

Often, I read inspiring, authentic stories about women, or men, who were brought to their knees by some devastating event or tragedy. Those moments either make us or break us. I have found the only way to overcome adversity is to surrender to it, not run away or jump over it. It appears we really find out who we are when the shit hits the fan. That happened to me too.

In 2003, we were a Kiwi family living in London. My beautiful elder daughter, Sienna, was born after a complicated and torturous 24-hour labour which failed to progress. She arrived by emergency C-section and I was delighted to finally meet her!

She was a dream baby growing up in those first two years. Sweetly tempered and affectionate, she coped incredibly well with travelling around the world with her parents, and the blessing of my eldest sister as her nanny.

My husband, Geoff, and I created and own an entertainment company based in London, New York, and Auckland. Geoff is a professional singer and qualified chartered accountant. My background is in PR, communications, and TV. From our business, we created the world's first opera band, Amici Forever, signed to a record label in New York. Geoff was singing in the five-piece group while I was co-manager. Both of us worked around the clock on a crazy schedule dictated by our various record labels in different territories. It was chaotic and exciting, stressful, and colourful. Sienna was along for the ride.

Because of my career I was not plugged into any mothers' groups, I was not exposed to other children, and I was blissfully ignorant of 'normal' developmental milestones. I had no one with whom to compare her.

I did note that Sienna had been growing distant and was not speaking enough words, according to age related milestones. After a final DPT booster injection at A&E, because of a playground accident, at the age of almost two years old, Sienna became angry, aggressive, and screamed the house down. I thought it was because her happy little world had been violated and she was responding accordingly. However, the screaming did not stop, it only became worse, and other awful challenges became apparent. She began to bang her head against a wall until it bled, and her sleeping became erratic.

She had terrible diarrhoea, her behaviour worsened, she would hit or bite herself. And her dream habit of sleeping through the night came to an end. She would spend up to seven hours throughout the night, for years, screaming for me, and wanting me constantly beside her. No matter what I did, I could not seem to provide the comfort she needed.

We went through an evaluation process with the NHS involving child psychiatrists, paediatricians, occupational therapists, etc. which lasted seven months. Only then were we given a diagnosis, or rather, a life sentence.

For a long time, I beat myself with a large stick - why did I not realise something was seriously wrong? Why did I trust 'experts' without doing my own research? Why did I waste seven months to find out instead of getting help immediately?

Why had I handed over my power to someone else, instead of listening to my intuition? But at the time, ignorance was bliss. I had been pregnant again, had just given birth to my second daughter, and was working for our entertainment business again in London (after resigning from our opera band to spend more time with my daughters). I was blinded by frenzied ambitious activity, like a good type-A personality. If I could turn back time, I would do things so differently.

Sienna was diagnosed with an autism spectrum disorder (ASD) in 2005. The team sat around in a circle with Geoff and me and watched us intently as the paediatrician informed us of Sienna's condition, telling us he doubted she would ever speak, fall in love, marry, or have children. She would be the family member we kept in the closet and her future would be dictated by how intelligent she turned out to be, which we would only find out when she was about five years old. The earth stood still. Geoff and I were devastated. I felt as if she had died. Everything I had thought about her was wrong; everything I'd hoped for her was gone.

I literally did not know what to do and no one in the mainstream medical world offered me any choices. They just handed Sienna a life sentence and told me to get on with it. Like so many other autism mums I hear from now, I spent hours on the internet reading and researching information and options. I was in shock and desperately trying to find a solution to help my girl, believing in my gut that there had to be a way I could do something for her, even when our doctors and 'experts' told me there was nothing I could do.

Geoff decided to leave our opera group, Amici. The band was at the height of its fame, two number one albums, successfully sold-out tours of Down Under, Asia, the US, and the UK. Geoff and I didn't want him to be at the mercy of the record label telling him to jump on a plane at any day or time, when no holidays were allowed and all activity was prioritized over anything else (including the births of our daughters). The other band members did not understand, they were not married, didn't have children, and they were not sympathetic. It was a difficult time.

Over the next few months, through our final tour, we met some amazing people who offered key pieces of the puzzle: positive action and most importantly, HOPE. Geoff's resignation from the group attracted a lot of media interest in NZ and Australia; the response was extraordinary. I am beyond grateful to all the people who contacted us then, and in the years since. It is the help, and wisdom, from other parents which has been the most priceless and valuable lifeline on our journey.

Through our media profile, I met a functional medicine doctor who had begun to investigate gut issues in children presenting with 'autism' and related issues, because her own children had presented with conditions deemed impossible to fix by the mainstream medical world, hence her personal crusade.

With the specialist's advice I cut out inflammatory foods such as gluten, dairy, sugar, corn, soy plus beef, fish, and pork from my daughter's diet. After I removed dairy, Sienna started to speak. Everything had to be organic.

We did a range of tests to investigate what was going on inside. We found she had severe gut dysbiosis, leaky gut, an underlying mitochondrial disorder, an imbalance of bacteria in her gut, high levels of heavy metals such as mercury and aluminium in her body, and the list goes on. She was sick, really sick. And getting her well again became my mission. My studying for a degree in ASD biomedical intervention was just beginning!

In hindsight, I believe Sienna was born with a vulnerable immune system. Environmental damage, including exposure to vaccination adjuvants, heavy metals, chemicals, pesticides and toxins, all caused her 'bucket' to be overloaded to the point where she couldn't cope anymore, and damage was done.

Treating autism is like searching for each piece of a jigsaw puzzle to complete the puzzle successfully, and every child is different. No one can tell you what pieces you need for your puzzle, you have to find out yourself by trial and error, depending on your child's unique needs and responses to each treatment.

There are well-researched and safe interventions to try which you can use as a guide, and you need specialist advice along the way for your child's specific case, but the parent is the only one who is best to judge what's working and what's not for their beloved child.

From the beginning, and over the years as we progressed through the healing journey, I doubted myself and my ability to help her.

I doubted my ability to find the answers. I felt guilty for being a terrible mother for causing this, and not fixing it, and not being perfect along the way. I was overwhelmed by the task ahead to save my child, on my own. Who was I? How could I be CEO and chief bottle washer of Operation Rescue Sienna – the most important job of my life, when I didn't rate myself? Or worse, when some days I hated myself, because I did not live up to my own high standards? I struggled.

I was sleep deprived, stressed to hell, working, looking after another child too, and organizing this rescue mission. I felt if I cried, I would never be able to stop. I could not ask for help because I was not good at reaching out. At times I thought I was going mad (which was probably the sleep deprivation!) I suffered mostly in silence. On the dark days I was on my knees in pain and fear, and I wondered how I was ever going to get up again. But I knew I had to; Sienna's life depended on it so therefore I would always get up. And never give up.

I researched, investigated, and implemented a number of strategies to get my daughter's health back again, which I put down now under five pillars of wellness, looking at our lives 360 degrees:

1) Diet & Supplements – removing the inflammatory, toxic foods (and kept testing this) and giving nourishing food, ongoing. Providing her with the vitamins or minerals her body needed (zinc, Vitamin C, magnesium, B vitamins etc.) and avoiding what was unhelpful (regularly tested) and this continues.
2) Detoxification – getting rid of heavy metals poisoning her body and brain (far infra-red sauna; chelation protocols, zeolites, detoxifying foods etc.) and this continues.

3) Environment – avoiding toxic chemicals in our household, in every room, in every way (household cleaners, air, water, food, beauty products etc) to limit exposure to harmful substances, as much as possible. Hard to avoid EMF radiation though these days but we did not use Wi-Fi in London, using hard-wired connection instead, and we still switch all devices and electricity, where possible, off at night.
4) Relationships – positive and supportive! The energy we emit affects everyone around else around us, so we surrounded her in love and hope.
5) Mind/Spiritual – meditation, prayers, music, nature – whatever spirituality means to each of us - and lots of healing modalities to enhance her, and all of us.

We have done Occupational Therapy, Brain Gym, Music Therapy, Hyperbaric Oxygen Therapy, Sound & Light therapy, speech and language therapy, Heavy Metal chelation and Auditory Processing therapy. To name a few! I have taken Sienna to chiropractors, osteopaths, kinesiologists, homeopaths, naturopaths, herbalists, nutritionists, massage therapists, healers and functional medicine / integrative health doctors.

For nine years, throughout nursery and primary school, I employed specialist and tailored behavioural therapy, called Applied Behavioural Analysis (ABA) for Sienna, with different tutors over the years. It's a tough job, not everyone was good at it or cut out for it.

Bespoke ABA, entirely tailored to her fluctuating needs, was able to teach her skills and life lessons and these were even more impactful as her health improved.

She could increasingly focus and concentrate on the tasks; from learning to tie her shoelaces, to speak, to hold conversations, to leave the house without freaking out, to understand emotions, to academic skills at school, to complicated 'theory of mind' cognitive and social abilities in later years.

I thought for many years that there would be an end to all this; that I was seeking a Holy Grail which was to 'recover' Sienna (i.e. eventually there would be no trace of medical or social issues remaining). However, I learned over time to respect her soul's path, and the unfolding of why she's here in this world. I learned we're always evolving, and the future is an incomplete equation. Our healing journey does not end, there is no destination to get to. We still live a clean and considered life, 15 years later as we are, down the track.

The path along the way has been paved with some magnificent change agents! She is in, what the autism world call, 'managed recovery' which means the loss of criteria to diagnose her on the spectrum. She is fully functioning, independent at high school and in life. She lives a daring life, full of resilience and risks, joy and excitement, friends, and fun. It's up to her to take good care of her health now, to enjoy all that life has to offer with maximum of impact.

And me?

It is like the quintessential metaphor of the little caterpillar, hiding and enduring through the chrysalis, and emerging as a beautiful vibrant butterfly. That sounds a lot more poetic than it's been to live through, but it makes a lot of sense to me, regarding my journey in this lifetime up until this point.

My daughter would assumedly be the caterpillar-turned-butterfly, but I realise now that this was the catalyst for my rising from the ashes too. I'm not glad this happened to me and I wouldn't wish this experience on anyone, yet it's been, in the end, positively life-changing for me. I used to hate people telling me, 'God doesn't give you what you can't handle' – shut up! - and, 'You should write a book about what you've been through!' I felt too confronted by my own opinion of myself and need for perfection to do the latter.

Over the years I have spoken about our journey in the media – on TV, radio and in newspapers, and at wellbeing seminars to raise awareness of options to help other families. We have had amazing feedback and gratitude to make the lack of privacy worthwhile.

Sienna has suffered bullying at school because her story is easily googled by peers. I am sorry and sad for that, and I hope that does not haunt her or limit opportunities in the future. However, as I tell her, we have helped hundreds of people by our honesty, transparency, and wholeheartedness. That does seem to help her feel better. I have assisted other autism mums, discretely, meeting and talking online or in person, writing down everything I did to offer them suggestions and possibilities, yet never forcing any advice on them.

Often, I wouldn't hear back from them again directly, yet I would find out later they took the information and acted on it for their children. I was afraid to write a book. It would not be perfect enough, I would open myself to ridicule, judgement, criticism (especially about vaccines) or I would just get it wrong, according to myself, and it was too painful to consider in every way.

Yet, from this road less travelled, and years of self-healing, I now understand I am here to serve other families – and particularly women - by offering them hope, support, compassion, empathy, understanding and information. I have learned that I'm a guide, a way shower, a truth seeker and an advocate, to lead people into the light. I am writing that book.

I can claim all this with confidence now and stand in my sovereignty believing it to be true. But even up until recent years, I've struggled with feeling invisible – like the song 'Mr Cellophane' in the musical 'Chicago' – because I didn't feel safe to be me, so how could I expect others to really see 'me'?

And yet isn't that typical of the dichotomy of our self-perception, or our misunderstanding of how the human experience works. As certain people in my life said, 'but you seem confident and determined, look what you've achieved in your life! I would never think you are invisible. To me, you are very visible!' and I would brush away these opinions of those close to me, used to seeing myself through the habitual ingrained lens of 'not good enough.'

My thinking was a prison of my own making and when I learned that, I was liberated. When I learned I was born 'good enough' – perfect, whole, complete – I was liberated. When I realized I have never been alone, always connected to Source, with the healing hands of the angels and spirit guides upon me to light the way, I was liberated. When I surrender, let go and let God, I am home.

Chapter 25 – Susan Smalley

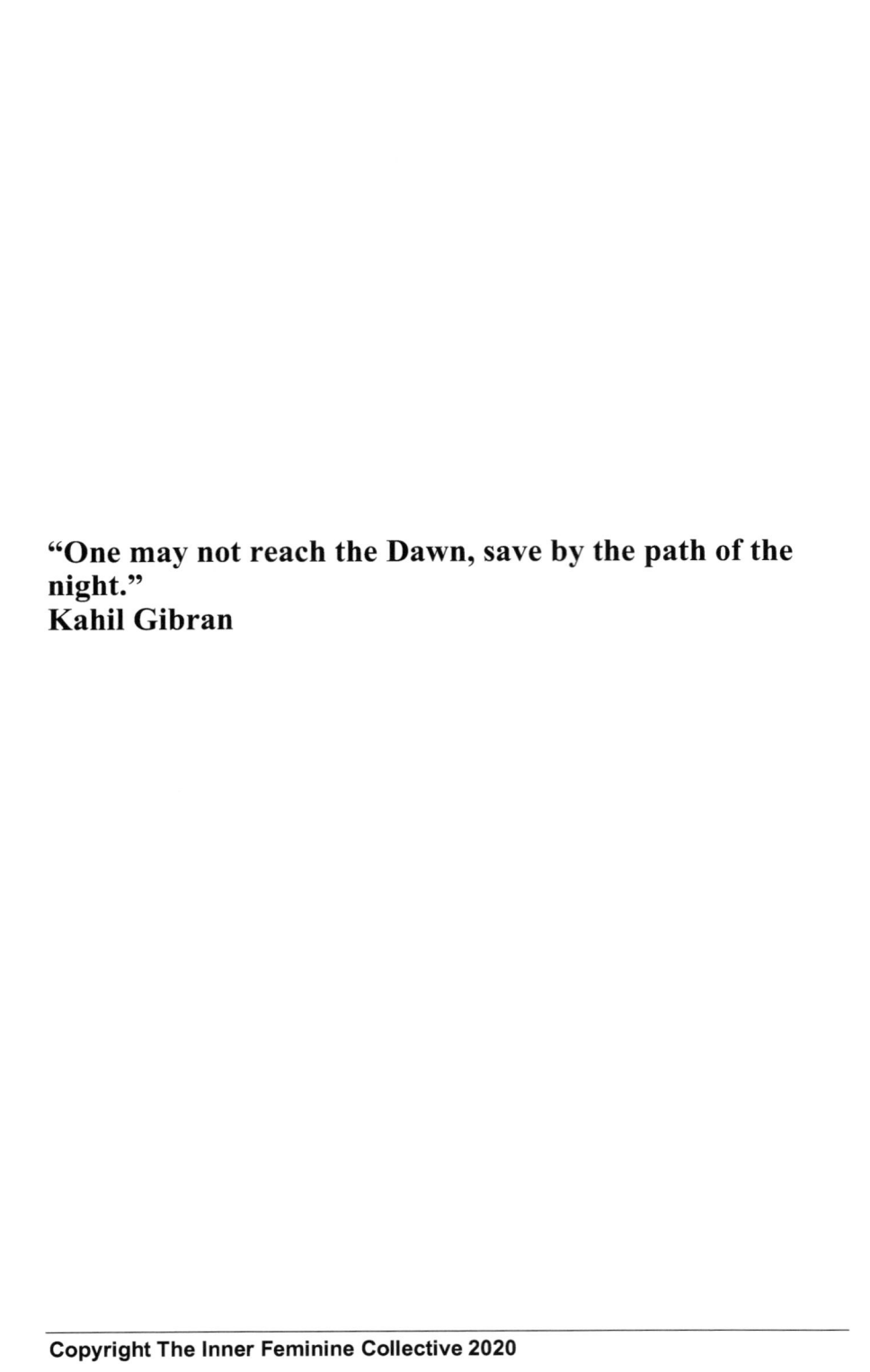

"One may not reach the Dawn, save by the path of the night."
Kahil Gibran

I am proud to have been born in leafy, historical, Durham City, with its meandering river, a host of beauty spots peppered throughout the county and an impressive Cathedral and Castle. I was born into the world at the edge of the River Browney, at 117 Office Street at 11.25pm on the first Friday evening of February.

Which is ironic, given I have spent the majority of my life working in *offices* throughout the region; holding the position of Secretary/P.A. to an International Sales Director of an import and export company. Working full time, but also working with the public part time, in the evenings and at weekends, psychically and spiritually, in my mediumship.

After 13 years I felt it was time I totally dedicated my whole life to the spiritual healing of hearts and minds.
Being a humanitarian trait of Aquarius, with seven planets in my fourth house on my birth chart, it is no surprise that my life path was to take me into a life of communication with people, and spirit.

I have such pride in every aspect of my typical Aquarian traits. Deep thinking and over analytical, gregarious in company and flamboyant in colour. Solitary and reclusive, innovative, and imaginative. I love being social, and interacting with others in my personal life, yet I defend my privacy and solitary confinement and spend hours swamped in books and study. I love travel and have always been the humanitarian for as far back as I can remember.

I love people. I do not like their dark drama. Perhaps because I have seen too much of it. I steer away from conflict and pain, and yet living a spiritual way of life, holistically, I have not fully succeeded in avoiding it.

A quiet, shy, self-conscious child, the eldest of three children, with three years between me and my sister, I have always been given responsibility. To organise and keep things flowing, not to be upset, or show disapproval. I was taught chores at home and knew how to skin a rabbit to pop into a casserole with pastry topping before I was at secondary school!

My Dad grew our produce, and supplied others in the village with his sacks of vegetables, which he carried down from his allotments, to the village crossroads, where, in the pub he drank in, others would purchase his prize onions, parsnips, carrots and swede. My best childhood memories are times spent with him and my Grandad Abe. At the allotments, just down from the gorse covered moors where another stretch of land, owned by them, was home to Dolly, a dappled grey horse, Prince, a black stallion, and Toby a chestnut brown pony.

I learned how to ride upon the back of Toby, saddle free and spent hours in the wild, running and trotting across the wild strawberry grassy mounds, down to the fresh spring waters my Dad knew ran beneath the surface of the moors.
He was incredible and when he came home from the pit, covered in black coal dust, his green eyes twinkling and his broad white smile beaming, I would hand him a mug of strong tea, and present him with a treat I had baked for him. My Dad knew the land, he knew how to get the best from it.

A prize winner, not only for his vegetables, but his huge, glorious flowers too. I suppose that is where my love of flowers and gardening stemmed from. Pardon the pun!

My childhood experiences saw me grow up fast. A turbulent start in life filtered into a lifetime of helping others cope with extreme difficulties. As harsh and emotionally painful as they are, I credit them with enabling me to be very aware of what people can be going through yet hide away from. I hear what is not said. I look beyond the façade, not in an imposing way, but in an intuitive reading of the energy vibration of the soul.

I recall being younger than four years of age and being aware of an 'unseen world'.

Being 'watched over' was something I believed and knew instinctively was the case, throughout the rest of my childhood years. Younger than ten years of age, I would hear a voice speak to me, see faces in reflections, and when in the company of adults visiting my Mother, I could sense their emotions, see their faces change, as spirit overshadowed them. I would know their thoughts and intentions.

I just 'knew' and believed that all my friends at school, would know too. I was soon aware that they didn't. I knew it was wise to stay silent about my ability. During teenage years at school, my school friends would confide in me, and I would give them gentle advice, to uplift them, if they were troubled at home, confused emotionally, or in despair because of troubles with siblings, parents or so called friends.

I guess you could say, I was a teenage *agony aunt*. Even though I was quiet and shy – others trusted me and not because of the way I presented myself out in the world, but because, as they often said, 'there was s*omething* about me.'

That 'something' was **a natural psychic ability**.

I felt emotions, even picking up thoughts of others. It was, I guess, best described as blending in with others, or '**tuning in**'.

Married at 19 years of age, I became a homeowner, which was quite unheard of in our little coal mining village five miles out of Durham City. I was quiet, private, and ever so proud of the home I had made with my husband. We shared the same outlook on life.

After five happy, secure years I gave birth to my only child, my son. I loved the pregnancy stage, I was totally wrapped up in ensuring he had the best early years, and I was a dedicated mother, stayed at home to nurture his development. I loved it! I studied at college two evenings a week, A level Law and A level Psychology.

My marriage ended abruptly. It left me in a spin. Young and attractive, I soon entered into a new relationship. An outward going, confident, adventurer of life, he was mature, fun, and highly educated. He stimulated my hunger for knowledge. It was he who brought me a little more out of my shell. He poured love into our everyday life together.

Our shared life experiences educated and expanded a part of me which had lain dormant. Traveling abroad, enjoying new exotic herbs and spices, wines, and cheeses, all contributed. He encouraged me to study, which I did with a passion. He honoured my love of mediumship.

He had had an imaginary friend as a child, and so was unfazed to see me take a deeper interest in the philosophy and science of Spiritualism.

For my first Christmas with him, he bought me a box of Tarot. A simple, plain deck of cards that sat for months unopened. If I am honest, I was a little afraid to open the box. But one day, equipped with a square of indigo blue silk to wrap them in, for protection, and quartz crystal, a flickering candle and a peaceful ambiance, I unsealed the wrapper, lifted the lid and expected all sorts of unbelievable weird and terrifying things to fly out from them! Nothing happened. I just held the cards unable to shuffle them. Unimpressive.

Some months later, when walking across the higher regions of Northumberland countryside, in Alston, I spotted a shop with a small long window dressed in all sorts of tarot decks, pictures I had never seen before. My heart began to race. I was fascinated! A slim dark doorway let me inside to a dark and dingy shop.

I was still very shy at that time, and I had to plead with my partner to go with me and ask the lady if I could purchase the long gold tarot deck in the window display. The High Priestess sat on the cover of the box and gazed at me. My solar plexus jumped and swayed, and my heart raced. Medieval Scapini. I loved the very sound of them! He made the purchase and I felt like I had the most treasured possession in the whole world right there in my hands.

I opened the pack discreetly. My eyes wide, sweaty palms, heart pumping; they emerged like new people into my life. New friends. I felt magic. A tremendous feeling of joy washed over me and so my love affair with Tarot began. The colours were gold, red, blue, green. Bright vibrant healing reaching out to me as I dived into every part of the imagery, clairvoyantly, to take a look around. I was fascinated. Hooked.

I have worked with Tarot for over thirty years.

Simultaneously, over twenty years ago I began to work on the rostrum of Spiritualist Churches and centres, groups in healing centres, and Mind, Body Sprit events. Helping to ease grief. Hundreds upon hundreds, seeking truth of life messages from loved ones in the spirit world. Being self-conscious, I found it nerve racking to stand in front of a crowd and speak. I remember how I was shaking like a leaf but then an immense confidence would flow through me while I worked. It was Spirit power of course and so it began. My mediumship lead magically into coaching others; teaching them about spirit - about their own spirit.

I worked every week, sometimes, three times a week in the Spiritualist Churches and have served right up until 2019. There was a great rift of faith that tore me away from this work publicly. You will read about it later.

I love that Tarot has never lost its magic, and increasingly teases me into further depth of knowledge about each individual card. I could never tire of its magic. It is the psychology of each card that keeps my love for it flowing and teaching others my knowledge, too

I have weaved psychic ability, or it has me, for nearly six decades, leading me into experiences with others. One such recent occasion was being led to a fresh clear soft sandy beach, to meet with a group of strangers, all dressed in white, in Northumberland, my second home, to give gratitude and set intentions for our lives ahead. Sparks of love, togetherness and respect flowed as we lifted up, quite literally, the bountiful moon. Whose illumination captures our imagination and stirs romance in our souls. The event was perfectly timed for me at a time when the road ahead was just about to change.

I did have some memorable magical experiences when I was a small child and my favourite story books were Treasure Island, Aladdin, Great Expectations Wuthering Heights, and Jane Eyre.

Magic adventures, miracles and mindfulness all governed by the twists of fate drama and romance. Yes! Romance - the total power of all life. I love romance.

Writing is a passion I love. Creatively flowing flash fiction, a little poetry, philosophy.

My total passion is memoir. I believe everything happens for a reason. Everyone in my life has played their part to orchestrate my next direction. I have of course ignored my intuition on the biggest scale you could ever imagine.

At the age of 50 years, I had only been married once. A relationship or two followed, both of which I drew amicably to a close. Both remain in my life, in differing degrees, still. Five years ago, saw I a turn in my road, I had never envisaged. Perhaps if I had, it would have been totally avoided. Someone entered into my life. I had never in my lifetime experienced a greater sense of security, trust, and respect. Friends loved him and often commented on 'how he was 'perfect'. My whole lifestyle with him was public knowledge, I shared on social media forums my happiness, as images taken together spoke to the world of the unbelievable love from the man who was everything and made everything so very 'complete'. We married in June 2016.

"I am so happy, I could cry." I said to him in July 2017. One month after our first wedding anniversary. "I promise you, this is the start, and babes, it is only going to get better!" his sparkling reply.

Three fabulous months later, my life shattered into a zillion tiny splinter. I felt like a first world war soldier laid in trenches with my insides blown apart. Blown into nothingness. In an instant I dealt with it privately. Softly. Amicably. I remained consistent.

Unemotional, level-headed, peaceful. I never raised my voice to him, despite the scream inside of my soul. I spoke peacefully and asked him *"why*?" He offered not one word of explanation. In true spirituality, I dealt with it, my way. Quiet, private, and non-volatile.

My trust and love had been based upon sand. Quicksand. I fell into an inner despair I had not ever imagined. I did not sleep, I could not dwell, I had to escape, yet I could not speak to anyone. My whole life was sucked down into the gnawing mouth of darkness. His soul was dark. He conned me. Deceived me.

I was rapidly unravelling inside. I immediately *shut out spirit* and became angry at God. **WHY!!!!???** Yet, an invisible thread, kept me breathing - Spirit.

I threw myself into my work, kept busy, addressed public meetings, worked online, coaching others, organising workshops, retreats, and gatherings for others in seminars and conferences. I pushed myself on and on and on, all the while, subjecting myself to more and more domestic abuse, mental abuse, emotional strain, heart wrenching pain.

Five long months in that abyss passed. I had so much inner strength, a power from somewhere out there too. I eventually consulted a solicitor. She confirmed what I already knew but did not want to face.

"He has conned you into marriage to manipulate you financially. You need to go home and ask him to leave." How sour humiliation feels.

He had planned it all, knowing that at the one year married stage, he would be entitled to half of my house, my savings, my income, and my pension! She advised me that I could prosecute him. My stomach turned. I felt nauseous, I wanted him out of my life, quietly, softly, and without drama. I filed for a quick divorce. It cost me just under two thousand pounds to do so. I wanted the nightmare to end. I could not prosecute him. I could not retaliate.
I do believe in Karma.

My mind was pulped. Daily. I dealt with this episode of my life as I had always dealt with trauma. Privately. On my own. It felt like the inner organs of my body were all twisted up within each other, like a huge expanse of giant toffee, churning and churning, spewed out from a machine that was his mouth, as it hardened with more and more as more revelations were uncovered.

I had to stay calm. I wanted freedom. In dealing with this trauma the only way I know how, I did so with grace and humility. In doing so, protecting him from public ridicule. I felt like Jesus did at his last supper. I felt the pain of crucifixion and kept my screams silent.

My divorce proceedings dragged out for nine months, NOT the six to eight weeks, it should have done, due to some inefficiency of the judicial system. Spiritual magic burrowed deep down inside of me within a grave.

For three years, I have grieved inwardly, taken no steps to smear his name. I have escaped from my responsibilities of work, coped with the stress on my own, detached and discarded all connections to him. Three months ago, I opened up again to the magic, with a rub like that upon Aladdin's lamp, whereupon a huge billowy genie appeared!

Spirit sprung forward and began to realign my life. Trust was re-gained, inner resolve restored. Confidence returning. I feel the magic again. This magic I do not give away to anyone. This magic is mine.

This magic is for me to fly upon, like a carpet, into whole new adventures into new places, with new people, and bring out the inspiration more and more. It restores my love of travel abroad.

My life is flowing once more. Inspiration restored so much; I have birthed twins. One new business of inspiration art, flourishing and flung out at rapid speed; and my voice has spread across the airwaves in my Soul Rising Podcast, interviewing others about their own life experiences where their faith and health has been tested.

I steer clear of lower vibrational situations, or people, and remain surrounded by light. In having gone through the darkest, bleakest, deepest bowels of my life, I have risen up and illuminated so many others.

I have eaten to fulfil an emotional pain, and have understandably, gained weight. Through what I have been through I am lucky to be alive, so carry it like a medal upon a returning soldier from a battlefield. With pride.

You saw me at the full moon gathering, all dressed in white. How proud and snazzy did you see me feel? White the brightest hue, upon a backdrop of jade and turquoise ocean, that day, even the sand was light and whipped up into a softness for me to walk upon. I gifted to myself, it was my new beginning.

White the colour of purity and spirituality. White the colour of transformation and change. White the illumination I feel my experience has given me. Spiritual workers like me, are referred to as 'carriers of the light'.

My true magic is **light**.

My life, an adventure again. I feel at the helm of a ship upon an ocean that carries me into new experiences, my spirit, the silk white sails and my soul - the very compass.

I have walked my walk and can talk my talk, with sincerity.

Love,
Susan x

Chapter 26 – Leanne MacDonald

"We came here as one and we live our human experience as individual expressions of that oneness; when we live life in harmony and not separation we connect to our truth."
Leanne MacDonald

I was asleep for so many years, living my life completely and utterly as a slave to my limiting beliefs about myself and life.

When I started to awaken it was as if I was opening pandoras box.

Slowly but surely, I started to unravel, become unbound, cut free and begin to float.

I felt feelings that I didn't think would ever be possible.

Years of living life as if I were surrounded by 10 ft brick walls.

Only able to see what was within that small space, knowing there was something beyond the walls but not able to get high enough to look over.

I lived my life knowing that there was something beyond the walls I was confined behind.

I sensed something far greater than me and my oh so volatile emotions.

I completely misunderstood my entire human experience.

Growing up I used to intensely feel other people's energy, but at the time I didn't realise it was coming from other human beings, I thought it was me.

I would suddenly feel an overwhelming sadness that made no sense to me at all.

That confusion was interpreted as there was something wrong with me.

Something I grew up to feel a deep sense of shame around.

Overnight I placed every other person on a pedestal and considered myself to be weird.

I aspired my whole life to be up there with everyone else, the normal people.

The energy that I felt from others was always confused as my own.

If I were in crowed places. I literally could not bear the energetic overwhelm and used to put it down to being claustrophobic.

Now I know I am not claustrophobic.

As a child I was always anticipating situations, I had a very strong sense of how things might play out.

I knew how people were feeling, as if I could read their minds, and I always had this feeling that I lived in a different realm to others.

I would watch people interact with one another, and they would be listening and buying into the story and words of one another, and I would be sitting there seeing the situation as clear as day. I was able to see what was triggering the people in the conversation. What their intentions were. I could feel their bodies recoil as they tried to communicate, with a false smile on the outside, but furious on the inside.

As a teenager this made friendships quite difficult.

I didn't buy peoples nonsense, I listened but I heard something different to what they would perhaps have liked me to hear.

I knew when people were being inauthentic.

I literally could not handle being in the whole drama of a friendship, so I mainly stuck to my own company.

I loved easy breezy friends, friends who just wanted to laugh and have fun and not talk.

I was not good at long term friendship because I found the energy of it all a drain.

Even now, if I sense anything remotely inconsistent in another human being, I take a step back.

As for so many years I had been absorbing the energy of others, I have grown to detect the right path for me very quickly and protect my own energy in the process.

This misunderstanding of life led me towards a 25 + year journey of rock bottom self-esteem.

It is so hard to be a human being when you sense EVERYTHING.

I used to find it uncomfortable being in my own skin, I didn't know how to respond, how to react, what to say.

I felt like I was emotionally volatile, people around me did. I was trying my best to make meaning of my feelings, thinking they were all coming from me.

Labelling myself as weird at such a young age massively impacted me, and still does.

The 'I am not good enough' label is one I drop and pick back up again from time to time; and will forever more.

Looking back at my teen life, there were so many attempts by my angels and guardians to try and help me make sense of it all, but I was knee deep in the story of 'me'. I was going to need something pretty spectacular to wake me up.

The spectacular came.

My life was stopped in its tracks and I had no other option but go within and seek guidance.

My grandma died several years ago, and she was always my guide in life, so of course she is my guide from heaven.

The day I reached rock bottom I said a prayer to her, I asked for help.

I asked her what I should do now.

I asked her how I would get through this.

I sat in silence at 5am in the morning looking out of my bedroom window and I waited.

The moment I invited the help in, it came.

I was fed breadcrumbs, that slowly but surely lifted me out of the sheer freefall and blind panic that I was in, and into a higher awareness of possibility.

I went from feeling trapped, to deciding that I was going to start making some choices.

When this rock bottom spectacular arrived, I had a new-born baby and an eleven-month old, as well as two beautiful older children.

I spent a lot of time waking in the night to feed the baby, so I did a lot of social media scrolling.

One evening, an advert for a webinar with Gabby Bernstein popped up in my timeline and I felt the urge to explore.

It sparked a curiosity in me, I honestly didn't even recall following her Facebook page, but here I was, signing up to a webinar about finding your purpose.

That evening I went down a rabbit hole.

Everything she said felt familiar, words I had heard before. I also had a very strong sense that my Grandma was pleased that I had found this webinar.

Gabby mentioned several books, one was A Course in Miracles, so I went straight to Amazon and got the book. I don't think I slept at all that evening, I just kept reading, being mind blown and then reading some more and being mind blown some more!

A Course in Miracles made NO sense to me, but I read it, page by page and it took me months.

I felt like I had stumbled on something that was going to help me make sense of life, but it didn't quite make sense of life just yet – but I knew it would!

My intuition during this time was very much carrying me, I was listening to the nudges, I literally had nothing to lose. I felt like I was being guided and no longer felt like I was fully responsible for running the show.

I was feeling a sense of joy about life.

When I first started to explore this, in one audio of Gabby's, she talked about focusing on the last time you felt joy, and I was stunned as I had no memory of my last time of feeling joy.

I had been feeling unhappy and numb for so many years I had forgotten what joy felt like.

Later that day I was watching my children play and they were running around and being silly and I felt it, I jumped up so happy to have joy back in my heart!!

I had super zoomed in on the problems I had in life and while mentally coping with it all, I had been missing out on living.

My life literally started to unravel. Some days it was exhilarating, some days it was painful, but I knew that if I kept following my intuition, it would all work out OK.

I was elevated to such a positive mental state that anything in life felt possible for me and I was excited about things once again.

I had so many lightbulb moments, realising that as a child and growing up the volatile and unbearable emotions I experienced was me being an empath and connecting to other people's energy without even realising.

As I followed my intuition more and more, it became clear that this sense of knowing I had hated growing up as I felt like a freak was in fact my guidance system helping me out. I literally wanted to run around telling every woman I could find that life was in fact wonderful and we are powerful, magical pure potential beings!

That reconnection to the Universe and my truth was bliss. I had clarity around my human experience and the energy of which had created my experience so far in life.

I started to harness my creative powers and tap into my feminine energy.

Something my ego had blocked, because of a belief that I established that I was not a girls girl, as groups of girls or women triggered every single limiting belief I held, and also I had a belief that embracing my feminine energy would mean burning my bra.

Our ego is so good at blocking out possibilities or helping us shape our stories based upon our beliefs.

The ego is literally the filter which our thoughts flow through, and are perceived based on past experiences. But our ego is not our truth.

Our ego is a tool in the creation of life.

The higher I lifted the veil on this, the more exciting all life's possibilities got.

I had been suppressing my feminine energy and truth for over 30 years.

It was covered up with layers and layers of hurt, pain, frustration, emotion, limiting beliefs but still it managed to find a tiny crack to shine enough light from to gain my attention. My truth, and yours, is that we are pure love and potential.

We exist as unique expressions, but at our core we are one.

Where one-woman adventures in life she creates a pathway for others to follow.

It is our role to constantly wake one another up.

For we all get lost in the story of life from time to time, even after we wake up to our truth it is a constant exploration and uncovering.

When I started to harness and consciously direct my energy into the direction of things I would love, I felt like a magician.

I had this level of understanding that had been intellectual, light bulb moments, knowledge uncovering, but when I actually stopped to see the role that I played in the creation process my mind was blown.

The energy behind all of life flows through me, and into things I see before me.

The power that we hold as women is unstoppable, it's a force.

As women we have this wonderful innate ability to nurture and understand people on a level that the ego cannot reach. We see the potential in one another, we see the pain in one another, we see the dreams in one another.

When women come together that force is undeniable.

As a collective we can learn valuable lessons and heal old wounds.

We can bring to the light our shadow self and release it.
When women come together with a pure intention of love it creates the safest space for all of the work to begin.
The work of remembering who you are.

Your truth.

The biggest transformations happen when you can sit, with a group of women who trigger every trigger within you, and with the intention of love you bring those beliefs about who you are, and what you are capable of, to the light and realign with every women there.

Realign with the truth.

For years I couldn't even look in a mirror because I felt repulsive.

I felt awkward and wanted to just peel off my skin.

I had no sense of self other than I was worthless and incomparable to every other woman out there.

I felt inferior, I put every other woman on a platform above me and went into hiding.

My ego protected my heart by building up a story of – 'you are not a girl's girl, you don't like hanging out with girls, you like your own company.'

But I was lonely.

So lonely and so sad because I wanted to connect with other women, I just didn't know how to be a woman myself.

The feminine flame had well and truly been dampened.

During my awakening I was called to start integrating with women, and it was both the worst and best experience of my life.

Worse because the emotional pain that I had to face feeling inferior was sometimes unbearable.

The best, because I was able to shine a light on all of the unhelpful beliefs that I held about myself and my capability, and slowly but surely become unbound, so I was able to fully connect to and realise my truth.

Our stories are our greatest lessons.

The conflict and pain we sometimes go through can be our greatest lessons.

They can lead us right back to our truth.

Our judgements are key to breaking free from the stories we find ourselves confined within.

When we judge we are in our ego.

I have judged, oh my days, my judging skills were en point!

Judging was my automatic response to my limiting beliefs, judging others made me feel so much better about myself.

Now when I feel any sense of judging occurring, I smile, as I know it's just an old pattern or an old story coming up for release.

But that realisation was a journey in itself.

Our life is one big journey, there is no answer, just adventure.

I am enjoying exploring and becoming more and more curious about the me I created and the me I would LOVE to create.

I am working on my beliefs, and every day I am trying to reconnect to my truth as much as I can.

It's not possible to live life 100% in our truth as the ego is very good at its job but intention is everything.

I intend to show love, respect, and non-judgment and to explore only my own path and decisions.

I intend to help others start their own exploration of life, and to begin the great unravelling of it all, so they too can experience this wonderful in and out sense of bliss that I reside within.

I am not perfect as a human being, I accept that, I know along my journey I will have more lessons to learn and more limiting beliefs to bring to the light, but I am excited for the experience not daunted.

The moment you ask for help and surrender it comes.
Since the day I sat and prayed to my Grandma I have been guided.

Copyright The Inner Feminine Collective 2020

I have been guided to opportunities; guided to heal old emotional patterns; guided to walk away from situations. I see people and their actions and behaviours as fascinating, most of the time!

I did say I was not a perfect human being.

But I am no longer impacted by the actions and behaviour of others in the way I used to be.

I know there is a choice of how I perceive it.

I know that everyone is just trying their best to establish their own path.

If there is something nudging you inside, listen to it.

Follow it and see where it takes you.

Take your hands off the wheel and let something greater than you come through and steer you back onto the track meant for you.

Start to write down your dreams and desires and begin to imagine them in your life.

Everything and anything is possible for you.

When I first heard this I was in debt, on my knees, losing my home, losing my mind and it felt like the furthest thing possible for me, but the unravelling of me has proved that wrong.

There is an energy flowing through you right now that can bring any dream or desire you have into your reality.

The stuckness you are feeling right now is an illusion, it's your own brick wall.

Be open to see what else is possible for you.

Start to explore the beliefs you have about yourself and your ability and try something outside of your comfort zone. You can do it.

Back yourself, trust yourself and listen to your nudges. If you were always on the right path, what would life look like for you?

If your current circumstances meant nothing about your potential, what is it you would be doing in life?

Exploring myself through soul inquiry was the most liberating and transformational turning point.

I feel alive.

I have dreams and plans.

I am so happy to have female friends and to share their journey.

I place myself in situations outside of my brick walls every single day, knowing that I am always supported, and always being guided.

Go and live your life.

Take that leap of faith.

Close your eyes and just jump into life.

Copyright The Inner Feminine Collective 2020

We are all here cheering you on.

Tons of love,

Leanne x

We would love you to join our Inner Feminine Collective Facebook community

https://www.facebook.com/groups/582527145981013

With love and light,

Leanne & Natasha xxxx

Copyright The Inner Feminine Collective 2020

A special thank you to the wonderful authors who shared their heart and soul within their story.

If you would like to learn more about any of the authors, you can contact them via the links below.

Penny Thresher
https://www.facebook.com/cornerhousecoaching

Cheryl Mercer
www.facebook.com/cherylfindingmyinnertruth

Natasha Holland
https://www.facebook.com/natashahollandphotography

Lucy Sheffield
www.writingfromwisdom.co.uk

Helen Bartram
https://www.facebook.com/blossomacademyuk

Hazel Carter
https://www.facebook.com/dancingintherainuk

Denise Saunders
https://www.facebook.com/PositivePathwaysDenise

Kirsty Pearson
https://www.facebook.com/flyingfeathersfamilywellbeing

Amy Whistance
https://www.facebook.com/AmyWhistanceHolisticWellbeing

Michelle Maslin-Taylor
www.michellemaslintaylor.com

Gemma Alexander
https://www.facebook.com/GABookkeepingNE

Jules Sutton
https://www.facebook.com/coachingwithjules

Kim Boyd
https://tropicskincare.com/pages/kimboyd

Jayne Holland
Jayne.jholland@hotmail.com

Claire Zorlutuna
www.instagram.com/claire_zorlutuna

Lisa Johnson
https://www.facebook.com/lvtholistictherapy

Kerrie Patterson
https://www.facebook.com/postbullyingmentor

Wendy Concannon
https://www.facebook.com/empoweredwomencoachinguk

Vivienne Edgecome
www.vivienneedgecombe.com

Leanne Taylor
www.instagram.com/iamleannetaylor

Mariella O'Brien
https://www.facebook.com/mindgardenyork/

Wendi May New
https://www.facebook.com/wendiwobblewildarts

Sara Calgie
www.thestartstudio.co.uk

Simone Lanham
www.sewellfoundation.com

Susan Smalley
www.susansmalley.co.uk

Leanne MacDonald
www.leannemacdonaldwellbeing.com

This wonderful project was brought to you by Spiritual & Well-Being Mentor, Leanne MacDonald and Visual Storyteller & Visibility Guru, Natasha Holland

- Co-founders of The Inner Feminine Collective.

The stories and words of each author were expertly guided by Life Coach and Mentor Penny Thresher.

Copyright The Inner Feminine Collective 2020

Corner House Coaching

Penny is a Life Coach, mentor, writer, and speaker based in Morecambe in Lancashire.

She lives in The Corner House, a former Victorian corner shop, with her husband Nigel, two cats and two Labradors!

She is mum to Zoe (25) and loves books, music, and cooking.

Her philosophy can be summed up in 4 words:

#Love #Kindness #Compassion #Connection

Of this book she says,

"Working with all the authors, editing their stories, and helping them share them with the world has been a joyous experience. Pure inspiration on every page"

If you would like to connect with Penny, here's how:

Corner House Coaching

Work with Penny to discover your innate well-being.

Email: **penny@cornerhousecoaching.co.uk**
Facebook: **https://www.facebook.com/cornerhousecoaching/**
Corner House Words
Copy writing, editing, proof-reading, writing workshops and coaching.
Email: **words@cornerhousecoaching.co.uk**
Facebook: **https://www.facebook.com/cornerhousewords/**

Leanne MacDonald -Spiritual & Mental Well-Being Mentor

Leanne is a mum of four living in coastal Northumberland.

She is passionate about awakening the pure potential within women so they can go on to experience a life filled with absolute joy and purpose. Woman have powerful spiritual gifts, that when drawn upon they can create magic and Leanne inspires women to connect to their magic, tapping into their pure potential to create anything in life.

Leanne shares a daily blog that shares her insights and downloads around areas including:
- Reconnecting to your natural well-being.
- Unleashing your magical creative power.
- Creating whatever your heart desires.
- Tapping into your purpose and bring more joy into your life.
- Actually achieving goals you have always wanted to achieve!
- Set yourself free from emotionally reactive decision making.
- Living a life filled with joy and purpose!

https://www.facebook.com/leannemacdonald11
www.leannemacdonaldwellbeing.com/blog

Natasha Holland - Visual Storyteller & Visibility Guru

"Hey! I am Natasha, founder of Natasha Holland Photography, visual storyteller, and brand developer. My ethos is to empower female entrepreneurs to attract ideal clients & bring their branding to life with beautiful, bespoke photography."

I love running my own business and all the creative freedom and opportunities it brings. I have had the honour of working with women globally for the last decade and have had my work published in many books and magazines. Travelling the world with my camera in tow, helping women from all walks of life is most definitely my muse.

My manifesto: to continue to inspire female business owners to maximise the potential of their business through creating beautiful photography that influences, connects and impacts on their journey to huge success.

Over the last ten years I have embarked on a spiritual journey acknowledging self-acceptance, self-love and worth. Peeling back the layers of negativity and pain created by my past. This has enabled me to not only think outside of the box but has given me the opportunity to use my experiences to connect on an emotional and empathetic level with my clients.

My advanced interest in psychology, human behaviour and body language guides me massively in assuring my clients feel comfortable and confident in front of my camera.

I want to feel their story, see their vision and capture it in the truest form, being mindful to break away from society's standardized expectations of an "Insta perfect" culture.

Being a mum of three children, it's my goal to be part of a movement to help, inspire, guide and impact change for women who need it. NOW IT'S OUR TIME AS WOMEN to help and support those who have been let down, those who have lost their voice and those who are ready to rise!

Be your true authentic self and embracing your story using it to motivate you in your next phase in life. Evolving into a woman, so unstoppable, a woman who will achieve her dreams and use her story to create movement.

Be that woman.

Love and light Natasha x

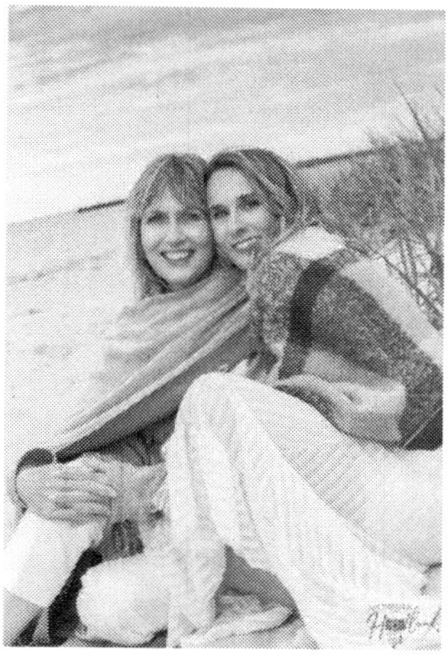

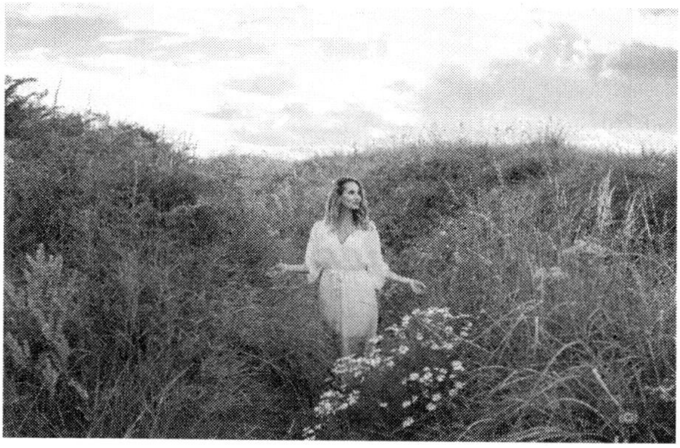

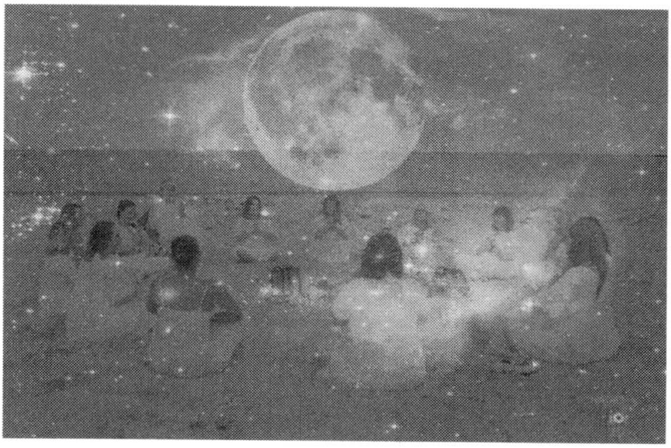

Printed in Great Britain
by Amazon